Contents

Straight Outta Feelings

(Political Zen in the Age of Outrage)

By

Stephen Kruiser

PREFACE

This relatively short book originally began as an unfiltered Facebook musing of mine. That in itself is unusual enough. I rarely post on Facebook and most of what I do is thoughtful bragging about my kid. Generally, if I am going to post something that just popped into my head I do it on Twitter.

I have been writing for a very long time and this was one of the weirder things I've done. It is more of a retroactive journal than a book. This could almost have been done as a series of columns or blog posts for a year-and-a-half had I only known what was going on.

When the first draft was done, I wasn't at all sure what to do with it. It had been a most helpful endeavor as far as figuring out the weirdness of 2016 and its aftermath from my perspective. It was just my perspective, however, and I pondered whether there would be any value in that for others.

I let it sit around for most of the summer of 2018 while I attended to some family business. Even though my original intent was to publish it I had an ongoing internal dialog as to whether I should or not that began even while I was editing it. I have a lot of internal dialogs – I'm not much for being around other people – but this one was standing out. Even though it's not a long work, it required a lot of reliving, remembering, and researching, so it took some time to write.

Many people had expressed interest in reading it, which is one reason I first decided to do this. I think most of them were expecting a rollicking, "Ha-ha" comedy tome, however. While I have tried to be witty whenever an opportunity presented itself, the goal of this was never to be one long crackup.

I was just trying to figure out how I became the one thing I've never, ever been: the level-headed calm guy in the room.

After a month or so of pondering I remembered that I am a raging egomaniac who thinks everyone wants to know his perspective on things. Even the ones who don't still often to like to observe me just to see if something really weird and self-destructive will happen.

Problem solved.

What follows are the recollections from a short journey taken by someone with an intense, longtime avocational involvement in politics who ended up in a place that he'd never worked towards or desired, but is greatly enjoying now that he's here.

There are going to be people who are offended by some of what is in this book, but that is unavoidable when writing about politics even in calmer times.

We are not in calmer times.

Well, I am.

Maybe some of that can rub off.

Stephen Kruiser

Tucson, AZ

October 22nd, 2018

PART ONE: PRIMARILY CONFUSED

ONE

The Walking Bad

I hate asparagus. Hate it with a passion.

Asparagus is the only vegetable that I don't like. I mean, I even loved beets as a kid, which makes me kind of a freak.

Even though I am a regular consumer of almost every other vegetable available in a grocery store produce department, people I know often take it upon themselves to become asparagus evangelists when they find out I am not a fan.

"But you haven't tried it *my* way!"

And I am not going to.

Because I hate asparagus.

No amount of asapara-lust from you is going to change that, and that is one of the greatest things about being a grown-up in a free society. We are allowed to experience the same thing in different ways. (For the moment, anyway. Academia is working hard to homogenize the brains of college students and change all that for the future, but that's another book.)

Let's practice something.

"To each his own."

"Beauty is in the eye of the beholder."

"Asparagus sucks."

See how this works?

There are so many adages about subjectivity because subjectivity is normal. If we all behaved and thought the same way we would be, you know, Canada. If Canada were real, of course.

***

Having been a professional stand-up comic for most of my adult life, I have an appreciation for subjectivity that many don't. People either love me or hate me. Rarely does anyone leave a live performance of mine with no opinion on my act.

My family is kind of the same way about me overall, not just my act.

We all experience entertainment differently, I just happen to have of a habit of not falling in with the crowd when it comes to many wildly popular things. It's not that I'm terribly discerning, either. One of the greatest things I have ever seen on television was a Japanese show called *Pan-kun and James*, which featured a chimpanzee attempting to do human things while accompanied by a bulldog. They make noodles. They go to an exercise class. They ride a train. Well, Pan-kun does, anyway. James is a bit of a slacker.

It was brilliant.

At least I thought it was. I have no idea if other people would be at all entertained by any of it but that isn't a concern. I don't need something to be enjoyed by others to enjoy it myself, especially when it comes to television. Most of my friends thought *Breaking Bad* was one of the greatest TV shows ever. Almost all of those same people are currently enthralled by *The Walking Dead*.

I subjected myself to two and a half seasons of *Breaking Bad* before I realized that it was never going to become for me the show that it was for everyone else. I began my stand-up career in the 1980s, so drug dealers aren't really edgy entertainment fare for me.

Three episodes into *The Walking Dead* I was rooting for the zombies only because I couldn't kill the painfully boring characters myself. After my *Breaking Bad* experience I had adopted a new rule that I had to find at least one character remotely likable before the fourth episode, so *TWD* and I were officially over.

These are merely two prominent and more recent examples. The list of wildly popular television shows that I couldn't stand goes on longer than an episode of *Mad Men*.

(Were they really only an hour?)

My daughter once accused me of being deliberately contrarian, especially when it comes to popular TV shows. (I'm sure she didn't actually say "contrarian" but it's a parent's prerogative to always imagine one's child as being exceedingly precocious.) As she is one of the few people on Earth whose opinion matters to me, I pondered whether she was right.

I don't think it is really true. When it comes to sitcoms I'm just kind of picky because I'm comedian.

The dramas that feature normal guys who snap and become dark anti-heroes don't do much for me because I got into plenty of my own trouble when I was a young man, so I don't need to live the bad boy life vicariously through a television character.

I'm also a rabid sports fan. Most of my groupthink participation as it pertains to entertainment is reserved for that. After almost thirty years without a World Series, I have an elaborate ritual for getting through the baseball season as a diehard Dodgers fan.

The same applies to the NFL and college football, and college basketball season just wears me out.

I don't have time to care about who zombies are after on Sunday nights, I've got games to watch.

***

All of this information about is meant to provide a backdrop both for how the 2016 U.S. presidential election and its aftermath have affected me, as well as how I've responded to it.

As the campaign moved into its seventieth year in August of 2016 and the emotions on all sides reached a screeching fever pitch, I found myself surrounded by an eerie sense of quiet and calm regarding politics. Given the fact that I am a bomb-throwing conservative opinion writer, this was rather odd indeed.

It crept up on me. There was no "Aha!" moment that I can point to where I realized that my experience of the campaign or election was vastly different than those of most of the people I know. It took some time for the feeling to hit me, and even longer for me to notice that it had.

It certainly wasn't a conscious decision. People who know me are aware that I can stay worked up about a variety of things for a long time. How I picked 2016 as the time to go all Buddha was a mystery to me at first.

This book is meant to be a trip we take together to figure out just what in the hell happened.

Have I given up? Am I too old to care? Am I resting up for a bigger fight?

I sincerely hope it is none of the above.

They are, however, not off the table as possibilities as this journey begins. Yes, I do have a theory or two, but I may not know until the I am done writing this what the truth is, if I manage to figure it out at all. (Spoiler: If you're reading this, I probably came up with something satisfactory.)

The way this is going to go is that I am going to recap most of the campaign and election as I experienced it. This isn't because I think everyone else needs a refresher, it is so I can figure out how I got from point A to point Z+++++ without seeming to hit any of the points in between.

Maybe I'm hallucinating. I may have begun closer to the end point than I thought.

I may be a Sim and someone is totally doing this for me.

I NEED TO KNOW.

Now all I have to do is cross my fingers and hope nothing sets me off before I am done here.

TWO

Please, Not Another "Historic" Election

The first two presidential votes I ever cast (different elections, I'm not a Democrat) were for Ronald Reagan.

I was spoiled.

As an idealistic young conservative, beginning my political life during the Reagan years wasn't exactly challenging. It was a bygone era, when conservatives could be vocal and proud even on college campuses without fear of "triggering" the more delicate among us. That's mostly because the delicate weren't really among us then.

The 1980s were basically conservative Republican Disneyland, with what we young right-leaning people thought would be a lifetime pass for fun.

Ah...youth.

My experience with the many presidential elections in the years since has been a mixed bag, to say the least. The heady days of my Reagan-loving twenties did not at all prepare me for the extremely crappy taste that settling for candidates would leave in my mouth in subsequent elections.

My first non-Reagan presidential election was 1988 and voting for his VP was a no-brainer then. By the time 1992 rolled around, however, I was experiencing my first bout of disappointment with Republican moderates. I stood in the voting booth seemingly forever, unable to decide whether I wanted to vote for George H.W. Bush or just leave that part of the ballot blank.

After about a day and a half, I opted for the elder Bush. Had I known about his sons I might have burned the polling place down.

I remember the summer of 1996, barely being able to keep from slamming my head into every wall I saw because the best the Republicans could do was nominate Bob Dole to go up against Bill Clinton. The GOP employed a merit system back then: if you lived long enough and weren't senile, you would eventually be given a serious shot at the nomination.

Bob Dole was such an awful candidate that I doubt even Bob Dole voted for Bob Dole.

Other than being spared listening to Al Gore's mushmouth droning had he won in 2000 (no, diehard lefties, he didn't), there wasn't much to celebrate from the beginning of Bill Clinton's second term to the end of George W. Bush's.

Then 2008 happened.

***

The American political memory is rather short. A lot of people forgot that the 2008 campaign began exactly as the 2016 slog did: with Hillary Clinton as the presumptive favorite to be the next president.

Hillary Clinton was so far ahead in early Democratic primary polling that the Democratic National Committee didn't even think of rigging the process to get her through to the end. That would be years in the future.

The Republicans obliged in keeping that fantasy alive, making it clear rather early that they would be sticking with their "next old guy in line" participation trophy nominating process. The late, great Fred Thompson jumped into the race for a while, giving some excitement to Republicans under 90. Sadly, after about four days of campaigning, Thompson remembered that he had a hot wife and emotionally checked out of the process, leaving John McCain, Mike Huckabee, and Ron Paul to vie for the affections of absolutely no one who cared. McCain was the oldest, so the other GOP elders simply barked "NEXT!" and he was the nominee.

When Barack Obama decided to pit his almost complete lack of experience against Her Madameship's overwhelming sense of entitlement, it took the Democratic electorate about seventeen seconds to jump ship for the new guy, largely because no one has ever really liked Hillary Clinton.

What followed Obama's ascendance to the presidency were eight of the strangest years of my life. Some of it had to do with his presidency, some of it did not, but we're on a political journey here, so I will concentrate on the stuff that did.

There was a lot bad, there was some good, and there was an overwhelming amount of, "Well I never said that at all."

Fierce Obama devotees were big fans of yelling at me for things I never said. Or wrote. Or even thought.

By far the most exhausting aspect of the Obama years was being told I was a racist every time I disagreed with my president. This was especially emotionally taxing because: A) I am not a racist, and B) I quite enjoy disagreeing with politicians, even the president. Also, prior to January 20, 2009, disagreement with the president was considered a right of all Americans.

In fact, from January 20, 2000 until January 19, 2009 the very same people who would soon disavow my right to disagree with my president repeatedly assured me that dissent was patriotic.

You can see why I say it was exhausting.

My friends on the Left (yes, I have many) employ nationwide teams of goalpost movers who are on call 24/7. An argument can begin over a very specific point but if you prove yourself right or the Leftist wrong the goalpost movers sweep in and change the parameters of the argument, the rules of engagement, or the original point.

That is precisely how dissent went from being patriotic to racist in less than a day.

Naturally, since there is now a Republican in the White House, dissent is all the rage (quite literally these days) again. Good thing for me, as the first budget of this presidency has been released and I'm not too thrilled with it.

All of that goalpost chasing was rather time consuming and tedious, even on the occasions when I was being paid for it.

Had even most of the normal rules of political debate remained in place from 2009 to 2017 I probably would have enjoyed it more. All of them, sadly, were abandoned by the Obama faithful in favor of employing character assassination. Gone were the halcyon days of them simply saying that we conservatives hated poor people. By 2010 we were all Islamophobic Klan members who wanted to kill grandma and Earth, but couldn't decide which to off first.

Did President Obama accuse us of all those things directly?

Not exactly.

He didn't need to, however. The press, long left-leaning and stealthily biased in favor of Democrats, abandoned all pretense once President Obama was inaugurated.

It began during the campaign but love was really in the air once he took office. I had been observing and writing about media bias for years at that point and I couldn't believe what I was witnessing in the early days of 2009.

What was supposed to be a press corps protected by the First Amendment in order to hold our elected officials accountable became an uncomfortable mix of swooning schoolgirl and totalitarian propaganda wing in the Obama years. One could easily imagine them scribbling "He's so *dreamy...*" and other love lines in their notebooks, dotting each "i" with a heart whenever they were covering one of Obama's speeches.

When class was over and they were left to scheme for his affection, they dutifully repeated any catch phrases the president and his team wanted to be circulated for narrative-building.

This, like many things I will merely touch upon here in the early stages of this book, is a subject upon which I've written quite a bit. It won't all be rehashed here. The media bias in the Obama years deserves its own book (or two) anyway.

Blinded by love, the media was more than willing to run interference for the administration. The president didn't need to call us Islamophobic racist murderers of granny and Earth, he had a press corps and the Opinion pages of almost every newspaper in America to do that for him.

A normal human doesn't spend his or her life proclaiming what he or she is not. When someone accuses you of being something you aren't, there often isn't a lot of evidence you can counter with.

"Look, here are all the times I didn't push granny off the cliff!"

It can wear one out after a while. Especially if one keeps taking the bait and jumping into defend oneself, as I did for far too long.

***

The rigors of defending myself against false accusations championed by media types who were emboldened by the fact that they were doing battle for a "historic" presidency were what made me dread 2016.

Mrs. Clinton loomed yet again on the horizon, but she wasn't my only concern.

One of the many things I was wrong about during the 2016 cycle was the fact that Hillary Clinton would be the Democratic nominee. I very publicly maintained that she is one of the worst candidates I've ever seen in my long political life, and I was convinced that Elizabeth Warren would eventually be drafted by the progressive wing of the Democratic party.

Yeah, I didn't see the Bernie thing coming either.

So, as the election talk was heating up in late 2015, I was firmly convinced that I would have to survive another historic candidate. I knew the Democrats would only have to slightly repackage their weak defenses of Barack Obama to make them apply to Elizabeth Warren/Hillary Clinton.

After eight years of being called a racist, I knew I was about to become a full time falsely accused sexist.

Had Michelle Obama been the one elected in 2008 we could have gotten all of that out of the way at once, but her fate was to fail miserably in her attempt to normalize kale for elementary school children.

I was going to be forced to try to explain to people that I am not a sexist, despite the fact that I've long said I would like to see a woman running the United States. Unlike my friends on the Left, however, voting for just any female in order to fill out a checkbox on the "historic" list isn't sufficient. It would be nice if America's first female president didn't have a body count or wasn't a socialist with delusions of Native American-hood.

My solace in the early days of the campaign was that the Republicans had a very deep bench and the Party of Youth and Diversity had a few elderly white people. The GOP could sift through a wealth of candidates for the ideal nominee while the Democrats held a round-robin shuffleboard tournament at the home to see who got the paper crown and an extra scoop of Jello.

That is how the 2016 presidential landscape presented itself to me at the time, anyway. Even if the GOP were to go on and win the election, I knew that I would, at the very least, be called a sexist seven hundred and forty two times a day until it was over.

I simply was not in the mood.

My mood didn't matter though. People were determined to go ahead with the campaign and election whether I wanted them to or not.

Yes, we Americans pride ourselves on being industrious, but maybe we should just take some time off every once in a while.

Or at least look into it every four years or so.

THREE

Night of a Thousand Candidates

Modern United States presidential campaigns begin around a year and a half before the major party conventions. For example, in March of 2011, I was asked to attend a presidential forum in New Hampshire that featured most of the Republicans who were serious about running in 2012 at the time.

(Now break off into small groups and discuss the insanity of this, then come up with ideas to shorten this painful process. All proposals must be submitted on half a page or less and with beer.)

Little did I know that the winter of 2015 would be the beginning of the end of my time as a Republican. I had been one since before I was old enough to vote. I was born and grew up in Goldwater's Arizona, we were just that way.

It was also the last time that I *enjoyed* being a Republican, even if those feelings of joy were intermittent and infrequent, at best. They at least still happened.

My flashes of joy were entirely rooted in the fact that the GOP presidential candidate pool was a wildly overflowing cornucopia that-GASP!-wasn't filled with people who were all retirement age.

For a brief moment in its modern history, the Republican party wasn't heading into an election year with its eyes resignedly and exclusively fixed on a grandpa in-waiting who spent most of his free time yelling to no one on the porch about the myriad ways that talkies ruined the movie business.

For those of us who had been busy as conservative political activists during the Obama years those were almost magical days. We'd experienced success in the two most recent midterm elections but were very desperate for the Big Win. We were all still stinging from watching a nice man but horrible candidate roll over and play dead in 2012 against a vulnerable incumbent.

Because American conservatives are duty-bound to spend at least half of our time engaged in self-sabotage (it's in the handbook), the bevy of choices also presented some ticking time bombs, but I am getting ahead of myself with that.

In early 2015 Barack Obama was about to get his term limit dismissal papers, the Democratic bench was just a row of rocking chairs, and the Republicans had a crowded field that featured not one but *four* candidates under the age of fifty. Optimism was the order of the day and we were all stocking up on extra sunglasses because the future was so bright.

Those given to revisionist history might not agree with me about the feeling then. I can, however, assure you from the perspective of one who was neck-deep in center-right American politics that it was a party. A never-ending, burgers-grilling, bottomless kegger on a sunny beach of a party.

Take me back!

***

There were, admittedly, some who were not looking forward to a primary with such a large field. The looming primary chaos that I was embracing was frowned upon by those who had firmly locked onto one candidate and would not be dissuaded.

While I had a decided favorite in the race, I wasn't permanently attached to the choice. Of course, I didn't want to see any of the Democrats win, but I was already perilously close to the point where that no longer meant I would automatically embrace the GOP nominee "just because."

As the non-Pataki field began to emerge in the early part of the year there were at least six candidates I could have gotten behind without feeling as if I needed a Silkwood shower every day between the final gavel at the convention and election day.

Again, this was more than eighteen months before the convention, when most candidates were still being coy and in the "wink-wink, nudge-nudge" phase where we all knew they were going to run even though they kept being noncommittal.

In normal election cycles the coyness is usually about assessing the other potential candidates and determining one's realistic chances (unless you're Rick Santorum, of course). This is where some attrition usually occurs, with a few prospective candidates dropping out before they're ever in.

As everyone would eventually find out, the 2016 cycle was anything but normal. Veteran political pundits and writers kept applying old scripts and conventional (no political pun intended) wisdom to the goings-on long after it became apparent that new rules were being written on the fly.

The first indication that it was about to get weird was the fact that almost none of the Republicans who were considering a run at 2016 were scared off by the prospect of a field so large they wouldn't all be able to fit on a debate stage. They all just got drunk and hopped into the hot tub. They even let Jim Gilmore in, probably because, like most of America, they weren't really sure who he was.

He did seem super nice though.

Whether it was measured in days, weeks, or even a few months or two, I do clearly remember but they were heady times for a Republican political junkie. The phrase "embarrassment of riches" was thrown around like cash in a hip-hop video. The excitement that an abundance of possibility like that brings made the atmosphere so electric that even Scott Walker smiled once.

Just the once.

***

Those emotionally or financially invested in a particular candidate were the only real outward drags on the possibility-induced euphoria that the rest of us were feeling. Hell hath no fury like a political consultant who actually has to work for his or her paycheck, and the mega-field the GOP was about to send out into primary season meant they were going to have to be doing more than just saying, "Let's spend $3 million on direct mail this week."

The bigger looming problem, however, was inherent in the very thing that was making so many of us enter the campaign giddier than a White House press pool reporter who had just gotten a smile from Barack Obama.

We were so busy embracing the multitude that we weren't being bothered by examining its components at the time. I may have been giving the individual candidates some thought but not enough to give me any trepidation about what was going to happen. The safety in numbers gave me false expectations of everything just working out, no matter who was in this early part of the race.

Put more plainly: I knew who the rock stars of the GOP were at the time and I assumed that one of them would prevail. I wasn't in the cult of personality business so, as I mentioned before, I would have been happy with any one of them being nominated.

As I also mentioned before, I got a lot of things wrong.

***

For example, I knew that Jeb Bush had a lot of Republican old money whispering sweet dynasty nothings in his ears but I didn't think he'd fall for it. People always did say that he was the smart one, after all.

Yet, even though he was eight years out of office at the beginning of 2015, Little Lord Jebleroy put on his best boy pants that were stuffed full of money that was still loyal to his daddy and attempted to wander back into political relevance.

Eight years in 21st Century politics is a lifetime and Jeb wasn't even the most popular Floridian in the race, so it wasn't like anyone was sweating him too much. His political accomplishments fading in the rearview mirror, all Bush had to run on was his name. Sure, there have been political dynasties and the two father/son president combos, but this is still America. If you try and sneak a third family member into the Oval Office it is going to start feeling a little too British-y for our liking.

What Jeb did to muck up the works was keep all of that GOP "Harumph!" money waiting in the wings far too long. None of it would commit to a viable Republican while George HW's boy was still in the race because loyalty or something. And stuff. Mostly a list of words that Republicans like to cling to when losing to the Bill Clintons of the world.

His campaign slogan was "Jeb Can Fix It" but "Jeb!-Just Because" would have been more honest. It also rolls off the tongue quite nicely when being chanted by a campaign rally crowd of two.

Please clap.

***

Nor did I foresee that John Kasich would become the herpes of the Republican primaries-flaring up when you least need him and impossible to get rid of.

Kasich's original value to the field was to provide Jeb Bush with some personality by contrast. After that, America was subjected to a year of this poor man's Columbo repeating "My father was a mailman," and "When I was in Congress," on a loop.

The problem with Kasich touting his fiscal conservative cred from his years in Washington was that he had been spending most of his time as governor of Ohio dry-humping every federally funded program he could get his mailman's kid's paws on.

Worse yet, he was fond of Jesus-shaming other Republicans as bad Christians if they didn't want to steal from taxpayers to prop up programs that would never actually get around to helping the poor.

Kasich isn't the only GOP governor in history to have begun on Capitol Hill as a spendthrift then moved into a statehouse and convinced himself that all money from Washington is "free"-he's just the most annoying.

His campaign was therefore built on a mixed message that railed against big spenders in Washington unless they were spending it in Ohio and then SHUT UP WHY DO YOU HATE POOR PEOPLE.

Kasich's hangdog shtick rapidly made him the most irritating candidate ever. He's the kid who reminds the teacher that she hasn't assigned homework yet, making even the nicest people in school want to give him a swirly in the boys' room.

Seriously Ohio, what the hell were you ever thinking?

Kasich hung around seemingly forever probably because he and just enough other Republicans thought he had a better-than-average shot at the VP slot on the ticket. Because the GOP refuses to put any effort whatsoever into becoming viable in liberal states again, most presidential elections come down to twelve drunk people in Ohio for them. Someone on the ticket from a swing state is one of only two Republican strategies for gaining the White House, the other being "We hope the Democrat sucks worse."

Have I mentioned that Kasich's dad was a mailman?

Because he probably just did again.

***

Scott Walker's almost immediate flameout was one I don't think anybody saw coming.

The guy had just groin-kicked the Democrats and all of their union money three times four years. He seemed invincible. He did painful, but necessary things for the betterment of his state. The Scott Walker in the minds of conservatives who didn't live in Wisconsin wore a cape and had super powers.

Sadly, one of them was that he could bore the paint off of the walls in a house six blocks away.

There were rumors of his less-than-dynamic personality floating around amongst Republicans who had only read about him, but we were dismissive of them. The guy just kept winning, he couldn't be all *that* boring, could he?

I thought that I had never seen him speak. The one time I'd given a speech in Wisconsin in recent years I had been at the Capitol with Walker's Lieutenant Governor Rebecca Kleefisch, who is a very good public speaker.

As I watched Walker during his brief appearance in the primaries I began to wonder if I had seen him, but had maybe gone into some sort of boredom coma that made me forget.

I'm getting sleepy just typing words about Walker right now.

Walker's early exit from the field should have been the only hint anyone needed to know that it was about to get super weird.

The GOP's greatest successes in the years leading up to 2016 came from the ranks of its governors. Walker was the most successful of a very successful group. He came in riding a wave of popularity that might have carried him through in a smaller field, heavy emphasis on the "might" there.

It became apparent very quickly that his polite, quiet demeanor was not going to serve him well on a debate stage that had more people than the audience. Honestly, Walker's wallflower debate personality may not have served him well even in a smaller field. He may be tough-as-nails when operating as a chief executive, but virtually none of that comes through when he is in front of a crowd.

Kudos to the voters of Wisconsin for seeing through that and electing him anyway, but the rest of us were yearning for more sizzle.

By September of 2015-more than a year before the election-Walker was already gone and, although they didn't really know it at the time, so was any real hope of normalcy for the Republicans.

***

Many of the more niche candidates had singular appeal for those not interested in the heavy favorites.

Lindsey Graham was there for the voters who wanted to keep terrorism front and center and needed a candidate who would probably start bombing ISIS right away if elected.

Chris Christie appealed to the northeastern Republicans who are really just repackaged Democrats from the 1970s. The portion of the GOP electorate that wanted a more acerbic version of John Kasich were drawn to Christie. Kasich's incessant repetition of "mailman's son" was swapped out for "former prosecutor" when the New Jersey governor was speaking.

Dr. Ben Carson and the Great Joseph's Grain Pyramids Traveling Road Show provided a lot of entertainment during the primaries. The brilliant surgeon was often hilarious when he felt he was being ignored during a debate and his opinions on things not having to do with his area of expertise were...yeah.

Rand Paul and his Dry-Look perm entered the race with what seemed like a lot of momentum. He appealed to all of the libertarians who don't actually want to vote Libertarian because they're obsessed with whether an "L" is big or small or medium sized. He made it into the 2016 portion of the primary season, but he lasted just as long as Rick Santorum did, which shouldn't have happened in a sane world.

Sen. Paul may have been the 2016 version of Rick Perry in 2012. One or two bad (or even mediocre) debates are almost impossible to rebound from in the television era.

Paul epitomized a problem that was inherent in having such a large field of candidates battling it out on stage and in front of cameras-the need to take one's personality up a notch.

Senator Paul is generally a very good speaker, but his is a style that can easily be drown out or forgotten amid a lot of noise, which this primary season certainly had. Like Carson, Paul is a surgeon. Those guys don't place a premium on being the loudest voices in the room. They may be precisely the men you want operating on you or a loved one, but not necessarily jockeying for face time on camera.

You can probably see where I am eventually going with this theory.

***

The last candidate we will look at from this circus before moving on to the elephant in the GOP primary room is Carly Fiorina.

Fiorina was intriguing to me for mostly personal reasons. I had given some indirect assistance to her ill-fated 2010 run for Barbara Boxer's Senate seat so I had some passing familiarity with her as a candidate.

That effort was ill-fated largely because she was an absolutely horrible public speaker and candidate back then.

I have no personal knowledge about whether she or the people around her admitted this, but I do know how much of a difference I saw six years later.

On a few different occasions in the latter part of 2015 people I respect were reaching out to me to tell me that they had just seen Fiorina speak at an event and that she had been amazing.

I asked each if he or she had been drinking.

Based on what I had seen in 2010 it was nigh on impossible for me to envision Fiorina captivating an audience.

When she began to emerge on camera a lot in late 2015 and early 2016 I was nothing short of stunned. She was better one-on-one. She was better in front of an audience. "Better" is a bit of an understatement here, actually.

She was transformed.

Carly 2.0 was focused and engaging, so much so I began to believe in pod people.

During the debate, Fiorina was able to keep a relentless focus on Hillary Clinton that the others were not. As a woman, she had that luxury of being able to attack Hillary without being called a sexist, and the males in the field still weren't even doing the bare minimum in that regard for the most part.

Fiorina did pick up a little momentum early on but couldn't figure out how to capitalize on it, and the best Hillary attacker in the field wasn't long for the contest.

***

There has obviously been one candidate not mentioned in this preliminary analysis of the large Republican 2016 primary field, and that has been intentional.

His entry into the race deserves a chapter of its own.

FOUR

Build A Wall Around My Heart

On June 16, 2015, an orange-haired Manhattan real estate mogul gave a most unusual announcement speech as he entered the race for the American presidency. Using a speaking style that had always been extemporaneous rather than relying on a script, Donald Trump threw a hat into the ring that almost everyone who paid attention to American politics thought would be thrown out sooner rather than later.

Oh well.

Trump's announcement speech offered a scathing report of the violent elements being exported from Mexico to the United States via a porous border. In Trumpian fashion, he went overboard made it seem like everyone who came here from there was part of the Sinaloa cartel.

Here's the thing though: he was giving a voice to something that most politicians in the United States had long-ago stopped talking about.

As someone who has lived his entire life in border states, I'd become infuriated by the narrative that every person coming across the border illegally was a plucky worker who just wanted to send money back to his or her family in Mexico.

There are a lot of bad people migrating northward from Mexico too. A lot.

The immigration debate in this country hasn't seriously been a debate for a very long time, mostly because no one is having an honest discussion about it, which was all I ever wanted.

While I didn't jump on what would come to be known as the Trump Train that day, I have to be honest and say his remarks didn't offend me. I had been waiting years for a politician to address the violence. True, Trump had handled it indelicately and went way overboard with generalization, but it was so refreshing to hear anything at all on the subject I didn't worry about that too much.

I am a native of Arizona, which has border issues that are unique from even those of other border states, so my perspective is different. I once lived twelve blocks from the border when I was a kid and woke up one day to find there had been a drug smuggler arrest in our front yard while I slept (I wish I could still sleep like that).

There are many in the southwestern United States who are single issue voters (I am not) when it comes to illegal immigration and they were all racing to jump on the Trump Train that day.

Most Americans weren't aware of this because so many had bought into the false narrative that nearly everyone was on board with a desire for "comprehensive immigration reform," a catch-all phrase that was easy to use to manipulate confirmation bias in polling.

When the people who didn't buy into that narrative spoke up, they were invariably called racists and thus became less vocal.

That, in a nutshell is how this whole thing got going in a very different direction.

***

Like most people, I viewed Trump as a mere curiosity in a race that I knew was going to be more crowded and different than any I'd experienced as an adult. Despite his clumsy honesty regarding the violent aspects of illegal immigration, I knew that I had little in common with him politically. I have a long-standing, strong distrust of northeastern Republicans and tend to be dismissive of them anyway. As I mentioned earlier,

I truly believe that they are all on a part of the political spectrum that probably would have made them Democrats in the 1970s. Largely because of that, I never seriously considered supporting him.

As for the border wall, I am not opposed to any suggestions about fixing the problem there, but it wasn't a powerful enough suggestion to move me Trump-ward at all.

There were, however, a handful of people whose opinions I respect immensely who were all-in as soon as Trump entered the race solely because they were single issue voters and he was the only one addressing that issue in a way that spoke to them.

Hindsight is a wonderful thing but, based on the history and evidence available at the time, Trump was an easy candidate to overlook. He is a successful man with an immense ego, and his run at the White House seemed like a vanity project that he was doing simply because he was restless and could afford to.

Despite the years-long protestations of the general public about being weary of politicians, most of us also already had a politician we were favoring for 2016. It wasn't difficult to keep Trump on the periphery of our minds even though there was so much noise surrounding him. It was early, after all.

That noise, however, should have been the overwhelming hint as to why he shouldn't have been dismissed by anyone.

A big voice and personality are needed to stand out in a crowd. Scott Walker found that out all too soon. Also, it doesn't matter if the personality is to everyone's liking, it just has to be an outsized one.

Perhaps a bombastic billionaire who also happened to be one of the most successful reality television stars in history shouldn't have been overlooked. Especially in the 24/7 media watch era of presidential campaigning.

Love or hate Trump, the guy does know how to command attention, both good and bad. If the goal is to pull the cameras away from your opponents, he is always the first one you should pick for your team.

The problem was that old rules were still being applied to the 2016 contest. Even the most experienced political people were still referencing campaigns of the past to predict how 2016 would go. There was no reason not to, even though so many things had changed in recent history.

Barack Obama's emergence in the 2008 campaign probably isn't given the credit it is due for signaling a shift in politics as usual. If you apply the old "Big Party Money" model, Obama shouldn't have been able to beat Hillary. Largely through social media and a new approach to dealing with email lists, he empowered small money donors.

This was something I wrote about a lot, but I don't like to toot my own horn.

It hurts my neck.

Just felt as if everything was getting too serious there.

Campaigns and parties used to ask their bases for fifty or a hundred dollars. Those were usually the starting points. It made everyone who didn't have fifty or a hundred dollars feel left out of the process.

In 2008, I was on the email lists of all the campaigns. The Obama campaign would frequently ask for just five bucks. There were days they'd be doing a fundraising push and ask for just three.

Everybody has three or five dollars to give.

Much of the outreach done for these pushes happened on social media. Hard as it is to believe for devout political types, the average American isn't on campaign email lists. Many are, however, on Facebook and Twitter.

While Donald Trump would use social media to his advantage in a very different way, what Barack Obama did in 2008 provided the groundwork for it.

None of this was crystal clear at the time though. Trump's road to the White House seemed circuitous, bumpy, and paved with layers of impossible back in those innocent days.

Sweet, sweet, innocence.

FIVE

Why Are Those Old People Yelling?

On the other side of the aisle, the field was decidedly smaller but still pretty interesting for any political junkie.

To the surprise of absolutely no one, Hillary Clinton had decided to make sure the two most ubiquitous names in modern American politics were kept afloat. Hillary vs Jeb was the dream ticket of all of the old party money on each side.

The old money may be rich, but they aren't very imaginative.

Hillary Clinton boasted an impressive war chest, the promise of another historic first, and didn't seem to have much in the way of challengers once Crazy Joe the Wonder Veep decided not to run.

The Democrats seemed content with pushing all of their chips in on a remarkably unlikeable candidate who they had soundly rejected eight years earlier. Rejected rather quickly too. As I write this almost a year after the election, they are still trying to figure out why that didn't work for them.

The problem with Hillary 2016 was the same as with Hillary 2008: she's not Bill Clinton.

Her entire political career has been built on the fact that she is Bill Clinton's kinda/sorta wife. She may be intelligent and ambitious, but if her destiny had relied upon her personality alone, she probably couldn't have risen much higher than an internship to the Hope, AR dog catcher.

Whatever desire most American Democrats had to get Hillary Clinton elected president had almost nothing to do with her and everything to do with her husband.

Democrats remember the Clinton presidency with extreme fondness and feel that his legacy hasn't been cemented because his vice president wasn't able to follow him into the White House. It is for this reason alone that they have given the exceedingly off-putting Mrs. Clinton a couple of chances to run for president. They have always felt that a win by her would be some sort of makeup victory for Al Gore's failure and give her husband's time in office its rightful historic due.

One of the reasons that it never worked is that Hillary didn't understand that this was their sole motivation. In her mind, everyone loves her as much as they love Bubba. Also in her mind: gallons of chardonnay. She always acted as if she were entitled to the office, which just compounded her personality problems.

Throughout the campaign, her handlers would try to rebrand and reintroduce her to the public in an effort to make her more appealing. They never grasped the simple fact that she had already had over two decades in the public eye to make people like her and, if it hadn't worked already it probably never would.

Hillary's unfitness as a candidate could be discussed for weeks and the exploration of all the reasons wouldn't be exhausted. It is nearly, but not quite, as long as the list of excuses she's been offering for her failure since the election.

On rare occasions, someone will get the urge to defend her worthiness as a political candidate and remind me that she won two Senate elections. I will then remind them that she only won the first one because Rudy Giuliani got cancer which, through some bizarre Clintonian pact with the devil, she probably gave him. My second reminder to them is the fact that being re-elected to the United States Senate as an incumbent doesn't require a lot of political acumen (see: John McCain).

We aren't here to figure out why Hillary lost, although we probably will revisit the topic later. We are here to figure out where I was in the process at each step of the campaign.

I wasn't terribly worried about the prospect of a Hillary Clinton presidency at this early stage because I was still convinced that she wouldn't be the nominee.

Bernie Sanders wasn't quite making his big moves yet and I was adamant that Elizabeth Warren was simply waiting in the wings, preparing to waltz into the race late and deliver Hillary Clinton yet another humiliating defeat from within her own ranks.

I live in West Los Angeles, tucked between Westwood, Brentwood, and Santa Monica. I'm not only surrounded by liberals, I'm surrounded really liberal liberals.

In the summer of 2013 (there's a picture of what I'm about to share on my Instagram account, I checked the date), I saw a car in my neighborhood that had a bumper sticker that read, "I'm from the Elizabeth Warren wing of the Democratic Party".

One bumper sticker does not a juggernaut presidential candidate make, but I am also in touch with my liberal neighbors and friends in the entertainment industry. Pre-Bernie Sanders, the word-of-mouth excitement was all for Fauxcahontas. And I mean all. I would have needed to take over an NSA satellite in order to look far enough to find someone who was looking forward to a Hillary Clinton nomination.

Clarifying: I didn't mean to imply that I know how to take over an NSA satellite.

As far as you know.

I was even less worried about an Elizabeth Warren run at the White House, which is why I wasn't really sweating anything then. She can actually come across more abrasive than Hillary. Both always seem to be scolding whatever audience is in front of them. Bernie gets away with the same thing because he looks like some crazy uncle yelling things at a barbecue while everyone ignores him.

Many will undoubtedly say it is sexist to give Sanders a pass while insisting that the two women are harsh while all three are behaving essentially the same. That isn't the case at all.

Bernie's disheveled lunatic shtick makes him easy to dismiss while he's barking at people. People take Clinton and Warren more seriously.

So, yay girl power!

***

While it turns out that I wasn't wrong about Hillary Clinton's complete unworthiness as a candidate, I was way off base about her staying power. I truly believed that the Democrats were going to have another 2008 moment, thinking, "Oh God, we can't go forward with this woman. She's just super unpleasant and stuff."

Then again, I didn't know that the Democrats had rigged the whole thing in her favor. I mean, even beyond the magical "super delegates" nonsense. Julian Assange hadn't yet brought us up to speed on that. The Democrats knew that Hillary wasn't an easy sell, and they would have to provide some primary cover for Her Imperious Scowlingness if they were going to get another historic first trophy.

They didn't want the smartest woman in the room to suffer another ignominious unseating like she did in 2008 and they obviously knew that she didn't have the skill set to prevent that from happening on her own.

They also hadn't planned on the wildest of wild cards showing up.

Elizabeth Warren had been commanding so much of the progressives' attention that Bernie Sanders, who had long been the standard-bearer for them, had been pushed to the side a bit.

Or so everyone thought.

It has been pointed out by many that Bernie Sanders and Donald Trump were opposite sides of the same populist angst coin in 2015-16.

At first glance, this is partially true. It was reinforced by the fact that both commanded huge crowds at their rallies, making it even easier to draw parallels.

There was a vast difference between what the massive Trump and Bernie audiences wanted, however.

The people who would eventually propel Trump to victory wanted jobs.

The thundering Bernie hordes wanted free stuff.

Bernie Sanders' appeal was built by promising to be a sort of political Santa Claus to gullible, math-challenged utopians, most of whom were pretty young. He's a political craigslist personal ad filled with lies. If he succeeds in luring you to the rendezvous point of his choosing, you will soon find out none of it is real and immediately regret your decision.

You will also lose all of your money.

But try telling that to a screaming throng of 30,000 millennials who think Uncle Nutso is about to wipe away their college debt.

As Sanders began putting together a string of these rallies, his bumper stickers began showing up everywhere on the West Side. I took particular delight in the fact that most of them were on vehicles that cost forty thousand or more dollars, proving that his supporters truly had no idea what he was talking about.

"If you like your Range Rover, you can keep your Range Rover."

The emotional shift from Lizzie to Bernie was on, and Hillary supporter sightings in West L.A. were still the rarest of rare things.

Bernie's popularity made it all the more difficult for Mrs. Clinton to avoid appearing to be irritated and entitled. Her smile became even less sincere, if possible. Pennywise the Clown from Stephen King's "It" was hitting her up for tips on how to make a grin more chilling.

The more stunning contrast though, was in relative appearance of health.

Sanders is six years older than Clinton, but always appeared to be more robust. Questions about Hillary's health abounded, and her frequent coughing fits didn't make them go anywhere. No matter how hard she tried to seem vigorous, her stooped, white haired elder always looked spry and more fit.

***

As the Democratic race began to shape up as one between a coughing grandmother and septuagenarian who screamed "OLIGARCHY!" all of the time, the Republicans weren't worrying about a thing.

They had all of those forty-somethings to provide contrast to the senior home on the other side of the aisle, after all.

Oh, Donald.

SIX

Wait, What?

The debates proceeded in a fashion that shouldn't have been a surprise to anyone: the GOP was a free-for-all and the Democrats were a mutual admiration society that occasionally erupted into genuine disagreement.

The Republicans spent most of their debates taking different turns at going after whatever Donald Trump's allegedly campaign-ending *faux pas* was that week. If one believed the party elders, the media, and conventional wisdom, Trump was a wounded animal as primary season actually began.

Add to that the constant chatter about Trump not having any ground game infrastructure, and it was almost a consensus that his was a doomed campaign.

A funny thing happened on the way to the ballot box...Trump started winning.

Not right away of course. Ted Cruz won the Iowa caucuses, which have been known to favor socially conservative, good Christian Republican candidates.

I will freely admit that the existence of the caucus process still baffles me, and I always smirk whenever I type or say the word "caucus."

The process does yield some strange results, though. I mean, Rick Santorum won there in 2012. Rick Santorum doesn't win anything anymore. He even loses most straw polls that are conducted with just himself.

Iowa 2016 offered a little crystal ball hint about the rest of the year that went almost completely unheeded. The quiet, conservative flyover country folks there propelled the bombastic New Yorker to a second place finish.

This was actually Ground Zero for When It All Got Weird.

Trump may not have won Iowa, but he didn't just go the hell away like the party wanted him to, either. Republican suits were hoping (some were assuring) that this would be the beginning of his none-too-slow fade.

When Trump did win in New Hampshire, it was still easy to write that off as an anomaly. It was a northeastern state that was familiar with Trump. Forty-seven people live in the state so who cares who they like? The most glaring reason to dismiss the results was that John Kasich came in second, proving that maybe those forty-seven people shouldn't even have the right to vote.

An emotional snapshot of this time would have revealed that almost no one in the Republican party was experiencing any worry whatsoever that Trump would prevail.

***

The primary season was moving into what was supposed to be the part where either Ted Cruz or Marco Rubio began to pull away.

The Cruz people had what they assured everyone was a solid southern and Super Tuesday strategy.

The Rubio people were running what I kept calling the Barney Stinson strategy. It was all a lot of, "Wait for it..." But they never told us what the "it" was. We were just supposed to know.

They also started to say "Florida" so often I was having Giuliani '08 flashbacks. I mean, another Republican wasn't seriously going to try and put all of his eggs in that basket again until they and his campaign turned rotten, was he?

If you are looking for something on the Republican side to point to and blame for Trump's rise, the deep animosity between Cruz and Rubio supporters should be Public Enemy Number One to you.

I was a Cruz supporter but could have easily voted for Rubio. I know only about twenty-five other people who felt the same way, and I hang out with half of them. We were most concerned with a Tea Party-esque Republican prevailing and were willing to overlook Rubio's "Gang of Eight" stupidity from his early days in the Senate. My circle tended to blame John McCain for suckering Rubio into that anyway.

We were most definitely in the minority.

Sadly, most Cruz and Rubio supporters had picked up one of the worst habits of Obama fans and were building up cults of personality around their respective candidates.

Worse yet, this division happened among people who from the early days of the Tea Party movement until the 2014 midterms had largely been working together. When it all began to unravel it had the ugliness of a family feud.

This had been an uneasy alliance from the beginning. The Tea Party years brought together groups of people who hadn't exactly been frequenting the same happy hours.

Beltway types and Republican consultants mingled with ideologue conservative activists like myself, and it was different but workable. I had been an activist for a very long time and had co-founded the first Los Angeles Tea Party but wasn't a professional operative. Many in the movement were new to politics altogether.

We were all thrown together for several years because there were a number of organizations that would hold large and small conferences. Many of these featured activists from the hinterlands (outside of Washington) like myself who would speak.

True story: most of us met on Twitter first.

If that camaraderie-of-convenience bothered the professional politicos it wasn't apparent. The conferences also tended to be one big excuse to day drink, which made it very easy to overlook things like minor political differences and budding resentment.

Then the media began lying about us all of the time, which provided a great bonding opportunity.

They seemed so happy.

We were storing political gunpowder for a fight we thought we would be waging together. We didn't know that it was just going to sit around unused and waiting to blow up in our faces in 2016.

My little trip in the Wayback Machine here is helping me understand that the Rubio/Cruz schism was inevitable but I honestly didn't think that at the time (the early Obama years).

I was still operating under the belief that we would all eventually overcome our primary differences to become the Anti-Hillary. For decades, the Republican standard operating procedure had involved a lot of sniping during the primaries only to end up with us coalescing behind a candidate that half of us felt uncomfortable voting for, but did anyway. If you think there are conservatives in America who actually wanted to vote for Mitt Romney or John McCain then you need to get out and meet more conservatives.

How drunk was I?

***

There is an old saying that Washington, D.C. is Hollywood for ugly people. As someone who has spent almost his entire adult life working in the entertainment industry while dabbling in politics I can assure you that this is true.

I can also assure you that political people are far more dysfunctional than showbiz types. After a few years of writing about politics and speaking at political events I yearned for the relative sanity of a road comic's life.

This part will alienate a lot of people I have known for years, but it's necessary because I probably should have felt alienated by them first.

There is an undeserved smugness that infects Beltway political professionals. They believe that they are the keepers of some secret knowledge about how politics in America really work and activists outside of Washington-no matter how experienced-are rubes.

Not surprisingly, the rubes bristle at this attitude.

That friction was the little seed that was planted in 2009 during the first Tea Party rallies and grew into a bitchy oak tree during the 2016 Republican primary season.

The great Rubio/Cruz Schism of 2016 was seven years in the making. As with most arguments that result from simmering resentment, it got ugly and personal in a hurry.

The Beltway folk and activists from the rest of the country were happy to work together to help Republicans during the midterm election victories of 2010 and 2014. As we all moved into 2016, that unity candle burned out, largely because the D.C. crowd didn't acknowledge the contributions of us rubes.

Let me be perfectly clear here: without the Tea Party movement and the activists it mobilized around America the GOP might have pulled off some whimpering midterm victories. The party almost certainly wouldn't have experienced the overwhelming successes they had for the Obama midterms though.

In January of 2009, the party proper was in full time wound-licking mode. Democratic strategist James Carville was repeatedly saying that the Republicans were about to wander in the political desert for forty years and there was absolutely no reason to believe that he wasn't right.

Had the party not caught lightning in a bottle with the mercurial Tea Party movement, we would all still be calling Nancy Pelosi "Madame Speaker."

By 2016, the establishment Republicans who weren't grandfathered into being Bush supporters were largely supporting Rubio. Cruz supporters were mostly grassroots activists who had an aversion to most things having to do with Washington.

Since Cruz's "I'm not here to play nice" arrival in Washington, the consultant class GOP had been more open about their hostility to the grassroots. It should be noted that almost every Beltway operative I know I met at an event being sponsored by grassroots organizations.

They were more than happy to party on the rubes' dime but unwilling to admit that we might be helpful.

These organizations may have been based in D.C. but were all about recruiting and training people from outside the Beltway to disrupt the old order.

Even though Marco Rubio had become the more mainstream Republican option, he may not have been an option at all had it not been for the Tea Party movement. He was the movement's first real success story. It was the grassroots activists who helped him buck the Florida GOP establishment and beat then-Governor Charlie Crist for the nomination.

Oh, how quickly they forget.

***

A gnawing feeling began being felt in the stomachs of both Rubio and Cruz supporters. Fears that neither candidate would even be able to slow-let alone stop-the Trump train were growing daily.

These fears weren't spoken aloud just yet, probably out of some superstitious belief that the mere utterance of them would make them all immediately real.

If you say "Trump wins!" 3 times he comes out of the bathroom mirror and tears your little Republican dreams limb from limb.

Rather than the respective camps focusing on what to do to defeat Trump, who was the frontrunner, they dug in and explored new ways to savage one another.

Internecine squabbling is nothing new to Republicans or conservatives. It's actually kind of our thing. A big part of the appeal on our side is that we aren't obligated to participate in a collectivist thought experiment that brooks no dissension. That makes for great feelings of individual ideological purity but it can often be the worst thing ever for winning elections or governing. Sometimes it feels like mommy and daddy argue over what to have for dinner every night of the year.

Sure, we would always find some way to force an extremely uncomfortable kumbaya moment at the end of a long presidential primary season, but that was part of the problem. The party felt comfortable with the "next in line" status quo because it knew that many GOP voters would just hit the bar and resign themselves to voting for a candidate they didn't like. Those who didn't would stay home, and the Republican would lose.

That's sort of an "if it ain't broke don't fix it even though it probably is broke" approach. The party elders were addicted to business as usual, even when business was failing. I'm not specifically referring to 2016 here, but to the general *m.o.* for the GOP in the last twenty years or so.

This frustrated conservatives the most, and by 2016 we were in the mood to burn it all down after the Romney Rollover of 2012. The friction between the Cruz and Rubio supporters would end up being what created the sparks to start the fire.

"Welcome to Survivor: Republican Island"

At this point the Rubio people were blaming Ted Cruz for Trump's success. Cruz didn't waste a lot of time during the early and middle parts of the debate season taking every piece of distraction bait that Trump threw at his opponents.

The Rubio people were asserting that, had Cruz attacked Trump earlier, it would have weakened him.

Team Marco really didn't think that one through all the way. For over two years they had been frequently portraying Cruz as a purely ego-driven politician who didn't understand how the game was supposed to be played. Now they were saying that he would have been the gamechanger, accomplishing what fifteen other candidates couldn't had he simply taken on Trump from day one.

They will dismissively deny that, of course. With smirks. Lots and lots of smirks.

Cruz probably remained the most viable threat to Trump by not wasting several months arguing about 24-hour news cycle noise that wasn't relevant to much of the electorate.

The division between Cruz and Rubio people began getting very personal, especially on social media. Activists who had worked and socialized together for years stopped speaking to each other, directly anyway. A lot of invective was being hurled from both sides, escalating mommy and daddy's dinner disagreements to the pots and pans-throwing stage.

With friends like those, who needs Democrats?

The sparks had hit the extremely dry wood of the Republican status quo house, and it was burning.

While that was going on, Donald Trump sat in a steel tower with a highly functional sprinkler system.

Seven

The Power of MAGA Compels You

When Donald Trump won the South Carolina primary and the Nevada caucuses in a three day span in February there was probably enough writing on the wall to specifically detail exactly how the rest of the affair was about to play out. Unfortunately, it was written in a special normal person ink that was only visible to regular, hard-working Americans who didn't bury their noses in political news all day, every day.

Those of us who should have known better knew nothing.

South Carolina was supposed to be the primary where either Ted Cruz or Marco Rubio stepped up and got things back to the old normal. They tied with each other while losing by double digits to the Manhattan Scourge in a southern state where he wasn't supposed to have a prayer.

On the other side of the country, Trump won in Nevada, which should have been the perfect clue as to just how long the Trump Train was. The "he won't be popular outside of the northeast" theory had been upended in a matter of days.

Deliveries of Pepto-Bismol and Xanax to various campaign headquarters probably tripled after this, even if brave faces were being forced all around.

The hopes, dreams, and delusions of the remaining candidates and their supporters were now completely wrapped up in Super Tuesday. There were nine primaries and two bearded lady caucus freak shows. Several southern states and Texas were up for grabs, so a lot of people were looking at Ted Cruz for a way back to normalcy.

Turns out it was Trump who had a southern strategy.

Cruz did all right as far as delegates went because he won Texas. More notable was where he didn't win: Alabama, Arkansas, Georgia, Tennessee, and Virginia.

Marco Rubio's "Florida or Bust!" strategy propelled him to victory in Minnesota so...you go, Marco!

***

This would have been a marvelous time for the other candidates to simply decide they'd endured enough sleeplessness and fast food and just pack it in. However, the political cognoscenti on all sides had convinced themselves that what was happening wasn't really happening. They may have been having some private night terrors where the truth got through to them, but the public line was still with "might" instead of "when" when looking at Trump's path to the nomination.

The Kool-Aid conventional wisdom about Trump was so strong that both Republicans and Democrats were drunk on it. One could almost hear the sighs, followed by variations of, "Why I never..." coming from smug-soaked rooms all over Washington.

This is the time that people were, at the very least, privately acknowledging that none of this was going to work out as planned. The exceptions were probably the people on the Rubio payroll. They were still operating under the fantastical belief that their Golden Boy would be delivered unscathed and via magic carpet to the Florida primary, where he would then be placed on a rocket ship that would propel him to the nomination through a wormhole or something.

If you dig deeply enough in any records kept from the campaign, I am almost convinced that you will find something similar to that strategy written down somewhere (but probably with more "Wait for it...").

Ted Cruz kept winning just enough to keep us interested, but we Cruz faithful were inwardly recalibrating our political emotions for a new paradigm.

I was still doing a lot of media at this point and I repeatedly said that if it came down to Trump and Cruz, the GOP elders of the village would back Trump in a heartbeat. Cruz had committed the political cardinal sin of not becoming an ideals-free invertebrate upon arriving in the Senate. Trump may have been a wild card, but Cruz had already proven to be a threat to shiftless, widening-derrieres approach of the Republican status quo.

That simply would not do.

If I were to pick a point where my emotional detachment began, this was probably it. It was apparent that what I had learned about politics during my decades of activism and years as a pundit didn't apply anymore. Unlike many in my position, I embraced that. I publicly stated that I would make no more predictions and left it to others to continue insisting that "normal" would prevail.

This is from the benefit of hindsight, which was the intent for this recapping of the primary season. I wasn't aware at the time that things were shifting within me, but it makes the most sense that this was the beginning. I had been at it so long that the emotional "Cruz can still pull this out," rhetoric was just that to me. My subconscious mind was beginning to do the work that would eventually result in an emotional liberation from politics.

Thank you, subconscious mind!

***

Kasich was still hanging around, but nobody was sweating him for the Big Prize.

The Rubio and Cruz people now began to put all of their eggs in one basket.

Rubio was obviously eyeing Florida, although even a win there wouldn't have put him in the greatest shape.

Cruz was hoping to maybe pick off a couple of southern or western states but the big dream was to win Indiana.

Generally, when a presidential campaign has all of its success pinned on one primary its days are numbered.

Trump kept having huge rallies, while the remaining candidates had huge complaints about

Trump. The former was resonating with the electorate, while everyone else was resonating with the media.

A good political rule of thumb that hasn't been blown to smithereens in the last few years: once a Republican candidate and the mainstream media are in sync on anything said candidate is in for an eventual rude awakening.

As Trump kept racking up victories and delegates, the political, pundit, and media classes were beset with what I like to call "Butch Cassidy and the Sundance Kid Syndrome." They (we) were mystified by the support and kept muttering, "Who *are* those guys?"

This was probably one of the last truly extended bipartisan moments in recent American history, as "experts" on both sides were equally confused. The more enlightened among us were just beginning to show signs of a Trump-induced apoplexy (Trumpoplexy?) that would reach previously unimagined stages of ridiculousness in the months to come.

The 21st Century has been one of rapid change in almost all areas of life. We ask our phones questions and they answer us. Noted online book retailer Amazon brings me my groceries now. Hybrid cars are so quiet you can get run over by one without having to go through the stress of hearing it bear down on you.

Given the "more, faster" nature of change, it shouldn't have been that surprising that American politics were shifting. Obviously, human beings weren't changing, but the way the voting public consumes information had undergone a radical shift in a relatively short period of time. The dozen years between the presidential elections of 2004 and 2016 may as well have been a hundred years apart. If you had talked about online fund raising in 2004 most people would have asked if you were concussed. In 2016, if you were under 70 and said that you had just "mailed a check" to a candidate you would have been asked the same thing.

The breathless hordes who in 2016 were getting carpal tunnel syndrome tweeting about politics were still contemplating whether to get a Myspace account to stalk an ex in 2004.

As people on social media are fond of saying: life comes at you fast.

***

Ted Cruz's Indiana Miracle play ended up being a double-digit loss to Trump, which prompted him to drop out and get back to work in the United States Senate. The Senate must have seemed like a Club Med vacation compared to the rigors of a presidential campaign.

Then again, the Senate probably seems like a Club Med vacation compared to even Club Med.

Cruz's departure from the race should have been all the hint the other candidates needed. Sadly, John Kasich didn't seem to be burdened by a need to govern the state that would eventually help propel Trump to victory.

More pathetic was little Jebster. Bush would eventually secure a grand total of 4 (FOUR) pledged delegates, proving to be one of, if not the, most spectacular failures in the history of American presidential politics given that he had so much big money behind him. His daddy issues kept him in for more than a month after Cruz gave up.

Donald Trump was going to be the Republican nominee whether the conventional wisdom crowd wanted him to be or not.

In elections past, this was the point where the GOP faithful would begin to rationalize support of the candidate. That rationalization usually involved just repeatedly muttering, "Well, he's better than the Democrat."

For a lot of us, that mantra had passed its "Use By" date.

Eight

Breaking Up Isn't Hard To Do

With Cruz gone, my election dance card was blank. Two days after he left the race I wrote a lengthy blog post for PJ Media in the style of a "Dear John" breakup letter, announcing my departure from the Republican Party.

At that point, I had been a Republican for my entire voting life but the relationship had been strained for quite some time. It would be inaccurate to blame Trump's ascent on the breakup (which people tended to immediately do whenever I mentioned it), but it is fair to say it was at least a catalyst.

I had long ago grown weary of voting for candidates I didn't like in presidential elections. Mitt Romney's nomination in 2012 almost pushed me out of the party but I knew that the bench for 2016 was going to be spectacular so I decided to hang around for one more quadrennial slog.

The real irreconcilable difference between me and the GOP was the Tea Party/Republican establishment friction I mentioned in a previous chapter. After 2014 I found myself being frustrated with congressional Republicans nearly as often as I was with Democrats. Establishment Republicans had taken the gift that the Tea Party movement had given them in the two Obama era midterm elections and told the gift givers to shove off.

A little gratitude would have gone a long way, but there was none. In fact, the establishment was largely incapable of displaying anything but contempt for the very people who had kept them in the game during the Lightbringer years. This ceaseless derision from people I find lacking in so many regards had already pushed me at least three-quarters of the way out the door.

When Cruz left the race I got my final nudge.

Again, this was more about the increasing distance between me and the political party to which I'd devoted decades of effort.

It wasn't me, it was them.

My feelings about Donald Trump at that point were largely ambivalent. He changed his mind on things so often during the campaign that I wasn't at all sure what he'd bring to the table as President.

I was not, however, of the opinion that he posed an existential threat to the United States of America. We had survived Jimmy Carter and most of what Obama had tried to do so I was sure that a President Trump wouldn't rip the fabric of the Republic asunder.

That wasn't enough to make me vote for him, however. I was done with negative pitches for candidates. "He's not as bad as the other one," wasn't enough to motivate me anymore. I explained that in detail in the breakup post I'd written and found out that I was most definitely not alone in that feeling.

The two paths for disgruntled Republicans who didn't initially support Trump quickly became clear: Never Trump or Never Hillary.

The former group was a hybrid mix of very moderate Republicans who loathed change and some hardcore conservatives who simply decided to invest themselves in disgruntlement.

They seemed harmless at the time.

The Never Hillary conservatives didn't call themselves that much but it's what they were. Comprised of mostly Cruz supporters and Republicans who just CANNOT EVER vote for a Democrat, they distilled the election to a binary choice and rationalized support for Trump.

This is where I hit a fork in the road and wandered off into the woods.

***

My path to political Zen began as soon as I hit "Publish" after writing the breakup blog post. Rather than feeling frustration about the upcoming election and my just-dumped political party, I felt liberated.

Nothing else had changed. I still had to pay attention to the news every day because I was still being paid to write and talk about politics. Most of the other people I've met who reached a place of calm in 2016 did it by checking out of politics altogether. I spent every day swimming in the cesspool but none of the stink was sticking to me.

I had no idea how this was happening, and I didn't expect it to continue. I simply wanted to enjoy it while it lasted. In the middle of a great first date you don't play out the entire relationship in your head.

I immediately changed my voter registration from Republican to Libertarian. I had no great affinity for the Libertarian party, but I've always been a libertarian-conservative. We differ greatly on foreign policy, for example, but I needed a new home. I couldn't register as an independent because I have maintained for years that there is no such thing as an independent voter. People inherently lean one way or another politically. No one is out there looking at just the merits of each candidate regardless of party. Anyone who believes they are is delusional.

So the Big L it was. Hey, the Republican Party and I hadn't been in sync on a lot of things for years; belonging to another party that didn't fill my entire checklist wouldn't be that difficult. I needed a place to park my affiliation until I figured out where I was headed in this big new political world of mine.

This was when tiny fractures in friendships began to appear. The fractures wouldn't remain tiny for long, but nobody knew that. It all seemed like fixable stuff. The binary choice stuff was leading to a lot of, um, spirited conversations among people who used to spend their time teaming up to fight liberals.

The seething animosity between the Cruz and Rubio people never got a chance to be properly vented because it was run over by the Trump Train. It remained buried for a few weeks and resurfaced for the big debate about taking one for the GOP team for just one more election.

"Debate" may be inaccurate.

Monkeys flinging poop at each other at the zoo are having more meaningful interactions than the Cruz and Rubio supporters were then.

Cain and Abel had a less hateful ending.

You get the picture.

***

Some background is in order here.

I first met Ted Cruz in 2011, when he decided to run for the Senate. Between that time and his election in 2012, I had the good fortune of talking to him several times, occasionally at some relative length. We were both speaking at an event in Dallas just prior to his runoff election against then-Lieutenant Governor David Dewhurst, who was the Texas Republican establishment favorite.

We were then both attending an event in Jacksonville just a few days after his victory over Dewhurst, and I got to spend some time talking to him on the way from the airport to the hotel because he'd generously offered me a ride so I wouldn't have to take a cab (my flight from L.A. connected in Houston, and we were on the same plane).

That night at the mixer that always kicks off these political conferences, Cruz graciously made time to speak with every activist in attendance who wanted to talk to him, even though he was visibly exhausted from the previous week.

Cruz was one Republican politician who wasn't afraid to give credit to grassroots Tea Party activists, and that alone endeared him to many of us.

If ever there were a candidate for me to back just because I wanted to finally participate in the cult of personality approach, Ted Cruz would have been the man. I genuinely liked him as a man, and his politics were very much in sync with mine.

During my busy activist years, I got to meet a lot of candidates and politicians though, many of whom I genuinely liked. Simply hanging out with them didn't mean they would get my vote right away and it never will.

Cruz was in step with most Tea Party activists and when he got to Washington and immediately made it clear that he wasn't going to play footsy with the GOP establishment just to make the chance encounters in the Senate lunchroom less awkward, he cemented support from a lot of us.

Despite all of this, I would have readily supported Marco Rubio had he become the Republican nominee.

The handful of Cruz supporters who felt this way were pretty much the circus freaks of the 2016 election cycle.

If there were Rubio people who would have supported Cruz, I never met any. That doesn't mean they didn't exist, it just means they were super quiet about it.

Keep in mind that those of us in the freak show often had to defend ourselves to other Cruz supporters as they repeatedly "screamed" "GANG OF EIGHT" to us in all caps on Twitter simply because we were willing to be flexible.

Speaking for myself, I was able to justify support for either because I have a lot of presidential elections under my belt and am never looking for an ideal candidate. Cruz was far and away my favorite in 2016, yes, but as I wrote earlier, there were a number of people in the field that year I could have willingly supported.

This is an important backdrop to what we will be eventually be looking at both for me, and for you, dear reader.

***

My experience in the political arena hadn't left me jaded or worn out, both of which might explain the detachment that I was beginning to feel at the time. It was my perspective from decades of campaigns and punditry that put me in a weird position in 2016. If I learned one thing from all those years-and this may very well be the only thing I did learn-it's that there is always another election.

Always.

The new people that the Tea Party movement brought into the world of political activism often tended towards a rather fatalistic view of the Obama presidency. To be sure, his "fundamentally transform" line didn't help matters any, but I don't think even he believed half of the crap he said. He was playing to his audience, which is what politicians do. All of them. That's how the whole "getting elected" thing works.

Many people, bless their hearts, really thought that he could, and would, hijack the republic in 8 years. What they didn't realize was that Barack Obama was far more interested in hearing the sound of his voice and looking at pictures of himself than in being the permanent head of a transformative political revolution. He prefers the more personal ass-kissing he can get from any slobbering late-night talk show host than applause from a throng of commoners.

In short, he wanted (still does, actually) to be a celebrity. There's a reason he and the former First Lady bought a house in California when they were getting ready to leave Washington.

For all of his progressive tendencies, President Obama was never going to fundamentally transform more than his ego. The United States would survive.

That was a hard sell to many of my conservative friends back then though.

The fear that one presidency could completely upend the Constitution and destroy America would turn out to be contagious, and truly bipartisan.

***

As I began carving a path to a presidential election as a man without a party or a candidate for the first time in my voting life I felt the first little bit of weight lifted from me. No longer would I have to compromise and put on a happy face for a Republican candidate who more than likely would spend whatever time he had in office frustrating me to the point of sever liver damage.

I hadn't rejected the idea of voting for Trump. I just didn't know where in the hell he stood on anything other than immigration. My gut feeling was that he wasn't going to govern as a conservative. Then again, Mitt Romney wouldn't have either, but I voted for him. Perhaps this all should have been worked out in therapy.

Although there was no concrete evidence for this, I believed that Trump might take a leftward turn as soon as he got into office.

The problem with having a non-politician run for the presidency is that there isn't any politician-y stuff to look at to get a reading on what kind of president he will make.

That alone should have had me sporting a MAGA hat but I was enjoying my newfound freedom. I was a political free agent as the primaries wound down and I was in the mood to be courted.

Gosh, I felt pretty.

At first glance, my remaining potential suitors all seemed like the political versions of a hairy-chested dude with his loud shirt unbuttoned to his navel and whose idea of showering was to empty a can of Axe body spray all over him.

But enough about Hillary Clinton. (rimshot)

It occurred to me that I was able to think about what I wanted from the candidates rather than being stuck having to adjust my expectations for the GOP nominee. That option was still there, but it was no longer my only option.

Adding to the Fellini-esque nature of my political odyssey was my continuing role as a political blogger and pundit. Almost all who were involved in either of those full time were already digging in and establishing positions that were defined by intractability. Lest I begin seeming as if I fancy myself some sort of pipe-smoking, above the fray observant philosopher type I should note that I am often given to intractability on any wide range of issues that extend well beyond politics. If you don't believe me, ask me about the designated hitter should we ever meet in public.

I not only wasn't digging in, I had no place whatsoever to dig.

After decades of finding myself in the exact same position at this point in a presidential election cycle I was now meandering through so much newness that it was as if I had been plucked from the most familiar surroundings imaginable and dropped on an alien planet.

Throughout the entirety of my politically active life I had mocked the very idea of "undecided" voters in the later stages of a campaign. Perhaps I had been a "binary choice" guy all along and didn't know it. Now here I was, in the waning days of the campaign leading up to the conventions wondering if I should perhaps spend Election Day bringing my own Crisco to a donkey show in Tijuana just to avoid everything.

I had become the object of my own derision.

Throughout all this time, I was still being paid to offering my political opinions. Such is the nature of politics. The only real opinion I had at the moment was, "Huh?" Still, there was a market for whatever "Blah, blah, blah..." I had to offer. There was certainly some pressure to move to one of the "decided" camps but I think my quirky "Heck, I don't know," phase had some novel appeal for the moment.

That wouldn't last.

Pressure was mounting on not just those in the political arena, but regular voters as well, to not only pick a side but be willing to commit to that choice as THE ONLY HOPE FOR THE REPUBLIC.

Undecided former Republicans (there was quite an exodus during the primaries) were told by former brethren that we were essentially traitorous malcontents who were guaranteeing that Hillary Clinton would be President for Life.

If we were talking to Democrats, they invariably insisted that we were, in fact, aiding and abetting the election of Satan himself. Because Democrats are the "Eternal Sunshine of the Spotless Mind" party when it comes to relevant history, they were complete unaware that they had been saying the same thing about every Republican candidate since Abraham Lincoln.

I had to make a choice soon, if only to be clear about exactly what kind of monster I was.

***

The contrarian tendency of mine that I mentioned at the beginning of the book was about to finally come into play. Of course, contrarians never think that we are being contrarian. My suspicion is that peeling the layers of our bad childhood onions reveals that most of us are just looking for reasons to remain apart from crowds we never liked anyway.

Cheery, no?

My political contrarian bent had been in full force for my entire career, of course. Being a conservative in the entertainment industry for as many years as I've been has gotten me quite used to having everyone treat me like a curiosity during an election year.

Now that I was in a position to buck what used to be my own party I felt rather relaxed and comfortable. I was enjoying the view from the outside now that I was on everyone's political fringe.

The only group I still belonged to was "Undecided" and that just wouldn't do.

Nine

The Rising Johnson

As I was no longer participating in a rote election year process I needed a plan for choosing a candidate I could vote for and do it soon so I could leave my undecided phase behind me as quickly as possible because I was beginning to worry that it might make me break out in hives.

I knew what my guiding ideological principles were. Those aren't very fluid for conservatives. Small government. Lower taxes. Strong military. The rest was mostly fluff.

If I ran the federal government the non-military portion of it could operate out of a single large warehouse somewhere in Virginia. I would keep the Capitol running mostly for the school tours and photo ops because that building is still glorious to behold, especially at night.

I also knew, and had known for many years, that my views were severely under-represented in this representative republic, even more so since I had become a resident of California.

There were the occasional bright spots over the years like Ted Cruz but, for the most part, we conservatives had long been people without a party, even while we were registered Republicans. Our time to hope that the GOP establishment in Washington would change in any way that benefitted conservatism had passed. I was one of the last to admit it. I can admit that now. As long as we're admitting things.

As an original Tea Party movement participant, I had been clinging to the hope that we could affect some change in the Republican party. My stubborn streak is as strong as my contrarian streak, so I held on to it far too long. Like a drunk slurring his way through pathetic pleas for one more round as the bouncer is dragging him out of the bar, I had hung around the GOP until I made a spectacle of myself.

Unlike the drunk, I didn't have the luxury of blacking out and not remembering any of it.

This was a critical juncture in my Zen-ward path in 2016. I had reached a point where I was distancing myself from the idea of voting for Donald Trump but, unlike just about every other conservative or Republican who was also rejecting the idea, it had almost nothing to do with Trump himself.

As I began to ponder just how frequently and thoroughly the Republican party had failed me, my decision to not vote for Trump was nothing more than a decision to not vote for any Republican.

The breakup was now complete.

My emotional tether to political passion was unraveling.

***

Shifting to a purely clinical view of the process, I now began to consider what criteria I would let guide me in making a choice for Election Day.

My chief complaint about being a Republican in recent presidential elections was that the party's main selling point for candidates was always, "He's not as bad as the Democrat."

It is a strategy that rarely works because voters aren't energized by a negative message. Something like that will probably do more to keep the "on the fence" types at home than get them to make a decision.

If you are a real Republican and/or conservative, the Democrat will always be a bad choice. The GOP higher-ups know this and have used that as perhaps their only real election strategy since 1988.

I needed something positive to move my decision needle.

That quickly narrowed down my list from criteria to a single criterion: the first candidate to say something I really liked got my serious consideration and, more than likely, my vote.

It should be noted that I was one hundred percent sure that Hillary Clinton would not, in fact, be that candidate.

Previous campaign statements did not apply, I wanted to hear something new.

Enter the former two-term Republican governor of New Mexico, Gary Johnson.

***

Governor Johnson was another politician I have had the good fortune of meeting when I was an activist. During my time doing online political broadcasts for the now-defunct PJTV, I interviewed Johnson three times from 2011-2016. Of course, we got to talk a lot before and after each interview too.

His reputation a very successful governor preceded him. Johnson was known to wield the veto pen to fight government waste more than any other governor before or since and that alone made me like him. The fact that he, like me, was from the southwest helped too.

We're an odd people and we understand one another.

A self-made millionaire who did it through sheer hustle, Johnson is far more conservative on fiscal matters than he lets on.

The issue he is not at all shy about is the legalized theft known as taxation. During an interview in with Reason.com in August of 2016 he said, "taxes to me are like a death plague."[1]

Boom, I had my one thing.

***

This decision was an easy one for me to make. I was very comfortable with voting for Johnson because I knew we were in sync on so many issues. Unfortunately, I only knew that because of my personal encounters with him. Admittedly, the online interviews I did with him weren't seen by a large audience, and only one of them was still available to view at the time. As a result, there wasn't much "public" to see and hear what I had from him.

I don't discuss my voting choices publicly too much, although there was never any mystery when it came to "President" on the ballot. Still, I treat voting the same way as I treat confession (I'm a Roman Catholic who actually still goes): what happens in the confines of the voting booth is my business alone. I'm not obligated to share just because

---

[1] http://reason.com/blog/2016/08/26/gary-johnson-no-to-carbon-taxes-and-mand

someone wants to get into an online pissing match on Facebook or Twitter.

Privately, I did let some friends and relatives know. Most thought I was only doing it because I live in California and my vote "didn't matter."

I have never taken that approach. If I ever do get to the point where I feel that my vote doesn't matter I will stop voting. Even in a state like California where the politics have been dominated by one party for a long time, the votes from the other side matter. It is important to remind the party monopolizing things that not everyone agrees with them. Since most coastal liberals and progressives never go near anyone who disagrees with them on politics, the votes are one way to wave from desert of political exile and remind them that we are still here. It may be nothing more than symbolic protest, but that is still better than apathy or resignation.

My decision would throw me directly into the increasing wrath of the binary-choice Republicans, but I knew that. I was now going to be faced with repeated variations of "that's just a vote for Hillary," usually delivered in all capital letters from people who weren't in any position to lecture me about politics.

Contrary me was now moving into his element.

***

My misgivings with the Libertarian Party, as well as with many prominent libertarians, were many. It isn't necessary to catalog them here, it is just important to note that we were not experiencing a budding political romance with one another.

I just needed a change and felt no obligation whatsoever to defend that change.

My freedom was already happening.

Man, did that piss people off.

The American zeitgeist of late 2016 was rooted in combative discontent. No one was supposed to be just OK with his or her choice for November. Your choice of candidate had to be the hill you were going to die on even if your choice was a concussed, heavily medicated grandmother who wouldn't be able to make it up the hill to join you.

I, on the other hand, was beginning to feel as if I had found my political beach and wasn't interested in looking for any hills on which to live or die. I wanted to find the cabana waiter and make sure he knew to keep the cocktails flowing.

My decided lack of misery prompted almost everyone who interacted with me regarding the election to crank their combative volume up to 11 to convince me just how wrong I was.

Naturally, the Hillary people were unhappy with me for the same reasons they would have been had I remained a Republican. That was never going to change.

The #NeverTrump people were unhappy with me because they had committed themselves to a permanent devotion to discontent. They didn't know that at the time and, sadly, they still don't. That doesn't make it any less so.

Although I can't prove it, I am sure that some libertarians were unhappy with me because I wouldn't talk or write about weed all the time now that I had sort of joined their fold. Here, I will write about it now: it's the most boring drug I've ever done.

But if that's what you want to make the center of your political universe, I am OK with it. I know that you won't ever demand that I die on any hills with you because there aren't any hills in the Taco Bell drive-thru.

Not surprisingly, the people who worked overtime to change my mind were the Trump voters. These came in two varieties, defined by their respective levels of enthusiasm and/or vitriol.

With the exception of only two people who I can think of, those who were on the Trump Train from the beginning now saw me as the Devil incarnate. To them, my one non-Trump vote was the linchpin that would virtually guarantee Mrs. Clinton a victory.

Even though it was coming from California.

I have been at this far too long to be lectured to by feverish, emotion-driven people who mistakenly presume that they know better than I do. Add to that the fact that it is my nature to be imperious and you can well imagine that these "conversations" were short-lived.

***

What few nuanced conversations I did have tended to be with Republicans who were reluctantly going to vote for Trump because they desperately wanted to keep Hillary out of office. It was the same old GOP shtick that I'd written about being sick of in my breakup post.

As with all things 2016, I was repeatedly told that this time the very fate of the United States of America hung in the balance if I didn't listen.

I didn't listen.

These conversations were generally with people who were originally Cruz supporters so we at least had that common ground. Perhaps that's why many of them were civil. At least the conversations with people I knew personally were, anyway. The binary choice Republicans who came at me online were usually less charitable.

Most of this crowd would at some point mention the folly of voting for a third party. This was an odd position for me to be in because I would have said the same thing at any other time before then.

Throughout my beating-my-head-against-the-wall activist years, I had adamantly opposed the idea of voting for a candidate that wasn't from one of the Big Two parties. My goal was to try and make the Republican party change to my liking rather than attempting to make a third party viable.

I had more success as a high school athlete than I did changing the GOP.

Fortunately, most of the people I debated this point with were unfamiliar with the fact that I would have been agreeing with them just a few months earlier. It is a lot easier to argue an issue without having to lead with, "Yeah, I was a moron."

Maybe having evolved on a political issue lends credibility to one's new position. I wouldn't know, because I don't do that a lot. I take great pride in not being blown about by political winds. I'd resisted this particular evolution for decades but had reached a point where I was battling my own party almost as much as I was the Democrats so I had zero guilt about changing this one long-held belief.

Like most Americans, I frequently complained about Congress and politicians in general. Unlike most Americans, I worked for years to try and get new blood into Washington, only to be met with derision and constant push-back by the old guard within my own party for whom the status quo was like heroin.

Throughout all of my years of fighting the status quo I was insisting that the two-party dominance should remain the same. I was taking a cafeteria approach to battling the status quo, choosing to only try and scrap one aspect of it while championing another. This is not unlike throwing out only half of what is in a smelly garbage can, leaving the rest, and hoping the funk goes away.

As big picture plans went, this one was about as unfortunate as my mullet in the 1980's.

Just like my mullet, this hideousness was never going away until I admitted that it was hideous. After a good look into a mirror that reflected thirty-plus years of futility, I loathed the look of two-party dominance in American politics.

My release from the bonds of caring too much about politics was almost complete. I knew that I wasn't going to change anything, but I couldn't keep complaining about processes in which I was a willing participant.

This series of mini-epiphanies didn't come until after I had left the GOP and registered with another party. I'm a slow-learner.

I was now on the receiving end of the very arguments I had been using against third party advocates my entire political life but I had something to throw back at them. If they became too persistent I would play the experience card and send them away.

I had taken one for the Republican team so many times that I could barely remember the last time I went to the polls with even a little bit of enthusiasm to vote for president. I could have considered doing it JUST ONE LAST TIME if I truly believed it would be the last time.

With experience, however, comes a highly functioning bullshit detector.

I knew I would be hearing this "one last time" pitch from these same Republicans for the rest of my life.

***

There wasn't much arguing on my part going on with the #NeverTrump Republicans during this transition phase. This is because they don't argue, they shriek, rend their garments and cease communication with anyone who doesn't agree with them.

The worst of this crowd were the #NeverTrump Republicans for whom one defining Twitter hashtag was not enough and who wanted everyone to know that they were also #NeverCruz.

Dogs who get locked up with each other during intercourse and freak out aren't as pathetic to watch as this group who were devoting so much energy to hating both Ted Cruz and Donald Trump.

Claiming to be the purist standard-bearers for conservatism and the GOP, they then went about attempting to prove this with a visceral hatred of the perhaps the most conservative candidate in the 2016 GOP field and complete rejection of the party's nominee.

As sales pitches go, this one was rather lacking.

What they didn't bring in the way of logic they tried to make up for with a stunning lack of self-awareness that made my Range Rover-driving Bernie supporter neighbor from earlier in the book seem perfectly understandable.

Even though I wasn't on the Trump Train, I was still a pariah to the Double Nevers (as I shall now refer to them) because I had supported a candidate who was no longer in the race but who was the scariest bogeyman in their political nightmares long before Trump.

The tantrums got to be a bit much for me. One quickly grows weary of people trying to replicate shouting on social media. Thankfully, I didn't have to put these tortured adult toddlers in a time-out, as most of them just blocked me and got themselves out of my way.

***

So, Gary Johnson it was, and I was sticking with that choice. All because he said he didn't like taxes.

It was the soundest reason I'd had for casting a presidential vote in decades. That realization helped me keep sailing on fairly calm seas for the remainder of the campaign despite the best efforts of others to roil them.

Ten

Conventional Wisdom

As the summer of 2016 wound down I was preoccupied with getting my daughter ready to head off across the country to begin college. This distraction should not be overlooked as a major factor in my lack of angst regarding the election.

While most of my political contemporaries were drawing lines in the sand and searching out new and often not very creative ways of insulting one another as convention time neared, I was moping in anticipation of being an empty nest dad.

I was in a bad mood, I just wasn't in the bad mood everyone else wanted me to be in.

It was well known for years that I was never a big fan of feelings in politics. I am, however, a sappy single dad. Leading up to the turmoil of 2016, I was mostly dreading my daughter leaving. Sure, I was thrilled that she had grown into a remarkable young woman and was off to run cross country and track at a great school, but I was a bit emo. I had joined a wine club and rescued a cat. As the summer wore on, I began talking to the cat more and more. He was actually responding to me in a more coherent fashion than any of the Double Nevers.

It is obvious to me now that I may have been liberated from an emotional attachment to the 2016 presidential election simply because I was focusing what emotions I had elsewhere.

That is a convenient theory, but probably not a complete one. We shall see.

Even if I'd had a candidate represented by either of the Big Two parties, the timing of the conventions was horrible. My daughter was on a vacation with her mother, so my empty nest feelings were getting a pre-season, if you will. Both of the conventions happened while she was gone and the cat and I were now having very in-depth conversations.

The Libertarian party had already had its convention. Or I think it did. It is unclear to me if the party ever has an organized gathering, as libertarians don't like to be told what do.

"*You're the keynote speaker tomorrow night, you should be there by 7 o'clock.*"

"*Fuck off with your time fascism.*"

"*Right. Got any edibles?*"

That's pretty much how I imagine a Libertarian convention to be. More weed, fewer goofy costumes, and a lot of people too baked to remember which state they are representing.

It does sound intriguing.

***

In late June and early July, the Republicans were preparing for their convention by completely losing their damn minds.

The party's chairman was expressing misgivings about the presumptive nominee's campaign. Some elected Republican officials were telling voters to go with their consciences, which was code for "Trump's icky." There was a movement afoot by several delegates to play fast and loose with the rules at the convention, mutiny, and back someone other than Trump. Some of the oh-so-concerned "principled" voices in center-right media were organizing theme cruises for their readers which promised boiling cauldrons and wiccan spells to rid them of The Orange Menace. And Metamucil mimosas, of course.

All of this was being done in the hope that the candidate who had gotten (by far) the most votes and won the most delegates during the primaries could be replaced by one who he defeated.

It wasn't a stretch to believe that the majority of the GOP heavy-hitters would be arriving at the RNC in one clown car.

The Democrats at this point were sitting back, laughing, and mentally shopping for Oval Office drapes that were thick enough to soften the sound of Hillary Clinton's cackle.

If any accurate history of this election is ever written, a significant amount of time should be spent looking at this lead-up to the Republican National Convention. As the party prepared for what is supposed to be the most feel-good portion of any grueling presidential campaign (other than a victory on election night, obviously), it was on the verge of fracturing into millions of pieces. The inmates were not only running the asylum, they were in a relentless search for ways to blow it up just when they were supposed to be celebrating.

The suspension of disbelief required to believe that any of the proposed alternative scenarios would be better probably would have set some kind of record if suspension of disbelief were able to be measured.

Anyone subscribing to the superiority of the Trump replacement schemes had to not only ignore the fact that millions of people had voted for him, but that they had done so with extreme enthusiasm.

The brain trust that was trying to oust Trump either never factored in what disenfranchising those people would do or, if they did, decided that a suicide mission was preferable.

Because hurt feelings.

They were, in short, engaging in precisely the kind of elitist snobbery that the coastal Democrats do.

"We know what is best for you peasants."

Fortunately, or unfortunately-depending on your perspective-whenever invertebrate Republicans attempt to behave like Democrats they aren't as adept.

The Democrats endured a populist uprising of their own in 2016 but, having learned from recent experience, put the fix in ahead of time to assure that Bernie Sanders' peasant revolt would be put down.

The Republicans not only didn't notice that the peasants were revolting, they kept pretending that it wasn't happening even once it reached their cigar smoke filled drawing rooms.

Put very mildly, I was happy to be out of that hot mess.

Because the only thing liberals are good at is whining, every Republican National Convention has a lot of protesters screaming outside of the gathering. In 2016, the convention had the added bonus of protesting coming from within its own ranks inside the building. That this party managed to make it to election day at all remains an American political miracle.

***

Donald Trump's acceptance speech was, predictably, roundly criticized by all of his growing legion of detractors.

As he had done throughout the entire campaign, he highlighted the real concerns of the portion of the electorate he was wooing, and not the coastal media people. These concerns were serious, and the speech was panned as being "dark."

As a conservative, I understand that reality is not always full of puppies and unicorn giggles. Trump's speech was full of reality, which is why the mainstream media was offended. They traffic in selling the liberal view of the world, which is not reality-based.

The darkness that the MSM was complaining about after the speech was the reality motivating the Trump Train voters. The media bubble people were too blinded by the lights from Hillary's celebrity concerts to see that.

***

To the chagrin of everyone except those who like to follow rules and accept the will of the voters, the RNC wrapped up with the candidate who won the most delegates in the primaries being named the party's nominee.

The horror.

Now it was time for the Democrats to sober up their nominee and take center stage.

***

The Democratic National Convention started off with a little acrimony of its own, despite the best efforts of the media and party power brokers to make it a happy affair from beginning to end.

As the DNC was about to begin, Wikileaks released a batch of emails that proved the fix was in for Mrs. Clinton from the beginning.[2] The pre-game of the Democratic National Convention was highlighted by the chairwoman of the Democratic National Committee resigning because it was apparent that she and the party higher-ups had been working feverishly to screw Sanders over.

The Democrats appointed Donna Brazile to run the Democratic National Committee. Brazile is a veteran Democratic operative who once infamously took to Twitter to ask why her health insurance premiums had just gone up. She did this just as Obamacare was taking effect.

Oops.

Still, she was an upgrade.

---

[2] https://www.washingtonpost.com/politics/hacked-emails-cast-doubt-on-hopes-for-party-unity-at-democratic-convention/2016/07/24/a446c260-51a9-11e6-b7de-dfe509430c39_story.html?utm_term=.3ff00f27a77e

The MSM diligently kept mentioning that the RNC was filled with dissension but this looked bad for the Democrats no matter how they spun it.

With this revelation, all hope that the Bernie Sanders supporters would just shut the hell up and acknowledge Her Madameship as rightful heir to the throne went out the window.

Sanders himself had become a dutiful pretend Democrat, spending weeks telling his supporters to transfer their allegiance to Hillary. It was a halfhearted sales pitch, to be sure, but was he was at least making some effort.

Even if the Wikileaks email dump hadn't occurred, it wasn't very likely that the Bernie supporters would go quietly into the night.

Sanders' entire campaign was built upon whipping youthful, clueless crowds into a frenzy with promises that no rational person could believe. It was a populist movement based largely on noise. The kids weren't going to sit down and play nice just because protocol dictated that they do so.

The revelations in the emails made even the adult supporters of Sanders angry. His delegates staged a walkout, forcing the press to twist themselves into knots to find ways to talk about Donald Trump while playing make believe at the DNC.

I won't lie, it was entertaining.

With the DNC kicking off from a clown car of its own, I can only imagine the Trump devotees thinking, "This is too easy." They had just survived every bit of nonsense the media and half of their own party had thrown at them and now the Democrats were going full, "Hold my beer..." to begin their own convention.

As the convention wore on, I was busy reading the media reports of what was happening and contrasting them with what I was actually seeing on television. The fiction pouring forth from the mainstream media was more reminiscent of a college freshman creative writing class than reporting.

All throughout the shaky beginning, reporters responded to the real turmoil in front of them by talking and writing about the RNC and barking, "Trump!" like trained seals.

Once the initial hiccups were quelled, the convention proceeded with the usual DNC formula: wealthy celebrities and wealthy Democrats (Kennedy, anyone?) promising to fight for ordinary Americans, as if they'd ever met any.

Of course there were celebrities. The Democrats always have celebrities. The mere presence of celebrities had been the primary Democratic political strategy since the Obama juggernaut in 2008. It is a flawed strategy when not paired with anything substantive, but the Democrats didn't-and still don't-get that. They continue to believe that all Americans are dazzled by fame. No doubt many are, but not so much when they've been out of work for a year and a Democrat is trotting out a singer with a lot of bling to appeal to them.

As it was a celebration of all things Hillary, they were obligated to let Chelsea Clinton speak.

Poor Chelsea Clinton. She got none of her father's charm or her mother's ability to frighten people into liking her. NBC had given her over half a million dollars a year to appear on television, an experiment which went awry even quicker than Bill Clinton's vow of marital fidelity. Viewers were muting her and waiting to watch the commercials.

Chelsea may very well be a nice woman. She is not, however, an interesting, witty, or charismatic woman. The reason that the fear of speaking in front of an audience is listed as such a great fear is that most people shouldn't do it. No one epitomizes that more than Chelsea Clinton.

Naturally, the press loved her.

By the end of the convention, the early week turmoil was forgotten. Or whitewashed. Bless the Democrats' hearts, when they want to put something out of mind it is *gone*.

I didn't watch Hillary's speech, I watched the celebrity reaction on Twitter.[3] Teenage girls at a Beatles concert were calmer.

With both conventions finished, it was time for the real fun to begin.

For me, anyway.

Eleven

Roadside Politics

The fifth U.S. presidential election of the 21st Century was supposed to be all about Big Data and the wiz kids who knew how to interpret it. Many time-tested approaches to campaigning were not only ignored, they were looked upon almost with disdain. After all, Hell hath no smug like a

---

[3] https://pjmedia.com/trending/2016/07/29/14-embarrassing-celeb-hillary-cult-tweets-from-the-dnc-finale/

millennial who has never known the loving touch of another person but thinks all human behavior can be predicted with numbers.

Predictably, Trump himself was eschewing the Big Data approach. Perhaps he didn't put much stock in it, or perhaps he merely enjoyed giving the press something to mock him about on the days they weren't just making things up. The Never crowd lit into him for this even more than the MSM did.

Team Hillary, on the other hand, was letting the wiz kids run wild. One older gentleman associated with the campaign repeatedly had his advice dismissed by the wunderkinds because it was so quaint and so 20th Century.

His name was Bill Clinton.[4]

The man who boasted a 2-0 record in presidential elections thought that maybe, just maybe, they might want to reassure the blue-collar voters who Trump was relentlessly campaigning in front of that the Democrats hadn't forgotten about them.

Using the "Low IQ Celebrities Are Threatening to Move to Canada If We Lose" method of predictive analysis, the Big Data geniuses determined that the election was essentially over and Mr. Clinton should STFU.

His wife apparently coughed her approval (the poor dear wasn't well at all) and the kids prevailed.

***

Around the time of the conventions, I had made it a point to tell individuals and audiences that I was done making

---

[4] https://www.nytimes.com/2016/11/10/us/politics/hillary-clinton-campaign.html

predictions as far as this election went. In all my decades of activism, I had never been so wrong about so many things as I was during the 2016 presidential primaries. A lifelong egomaniac, even I was no longer impressed by my powers of political analysis.

The safe bet was to not make any bets.

The problem with this attitude, however, was that it was still part of my job to write and speak about my political opinions. People paying for this quickly grow weary of, "Hell, I don't know," as a response and demand an occasional specific or two.

As I wasn't involved in any campaign home stretch activities for this election I had time to ponder. My daughter was now going to college on the other end of the country and a sports bar opened fifty yards from my front door just about the same time she left.

It was Pondering Central. Thinking about all of this with a good buzz couldn't possibly yield worse results than doing it sober had, so I picked my favorite stool in the new place and let them get to know me.

The previous eighteen months now needed a thorough going-over by me to see if there were any lessons that could be gleaned that might come in handy at the end of this mostly insane election cycle.

***

Speaking of insane, another aside about the Republicans is in order here.

After the convention, the #NeverTrump horde was not gracefully accepting the complete failure of their utterly ridiculous coup attempts. Like almost every other individual or group who had done something stupid during the campaign, they decided to double down on the failure rather than simply throw up their hands and wait to see how it all turned out.

A contingent of #NeverTrump GOP consultants and activists, led mostly by some Double Nevers, decided to find an eleventh hour (relatively speaking, of course) candidate to present as a true conservative alternative to Donald Trump.

The thought of mainstream Republican consultants who had forged an identity around hating Ted Cruz long before they began hating Donald Trump believing that they knew what's best for conservatives was (and still is) put very mildly, fucking absurd.

However, an echo chamber is the same whether it is on the left or right, and they were busy convincing themselves of the righteousness of their latest ploy. In typical consultant class fashion, they managed to be condescending while acting like the village madmen. Madwomen. Madpersons.

Lunatics.

Into the extremely noisy election fray of late 2016 was thrown one Evan McMullin, a former CIA operative who almost no one had heard of, as is often the case with spies.

Yes, the vaunted "We Know Best" crowd of the Republican party thought that an almost personality-free former spy would be the guy to shake up the 2016 circus.

When I say personality-free, do remember that this was in an election cycle that had already featured the walking insomnia cures John Kasich, Jeb Bush, Martin O'Malley and Scott Walker, all of whom were the epitome of effervescence when compared to McMullin.

McMullin's handlers decided to introduce him to the public via a TEDx Talk he had given earlier in 2016. I tried to watch it and almost immediately I could only focus on how painfully dry his speaking style was.

This is why you don't see a lot of CIA operatives going into stand-up or vice-versa.

The GOP power brokers have long struggled with firmly understanding optics. The general thought process is, "Hey, we have the better ideas, so the presentation doesn't really matter."

That's plausible if one has never heard of television or the Internet.

It was obvious that the Scott Walker lesson had not been learned by those attempting to create a magical replacement for Trump almost out of whole cloth.

Donald Trump was a lot of things during the campaign of 2016, but boring was never one of them. It was almost as if the McMullin people had decided to go with the complete opposite of Trump in every way, including the ability to connect with an audience. The only people who Evan McMullin would connect with would be those who had already decided that they wanted to like Evan McMullin.

He was bald too, another contrast to the oddly-maned Trump.

I wouldn't even be writing about this sad chapter in the race had it only been a protest move on the part of the anti-Trump factions within the Republican party. That would have been rational and understandable.

Instead, those of us who refused to believe that Donald Trump's mere presence in the race signaled the end of the American Experiment were subjected to what the McMullin supporters swore was a very realistic scenario in which he could win the presidency. It involved Trump winning some states he wasn't supposed to, which in turn would mean neither he or Hillary would reach 270 electoral votes.

This scenario also hinged upon McMullin winning his native state of Utah, which we were told by the fevered Nevers was totally plausible. Among the reasons given for Utah being in play for McMullin was that he is Mormon.

That's right, conservatives were supposed to save themselves by stooping to identity politics.

Once the above objectives were accomplished, the rest was fairly simple to understand for those who have even a rudimentary grasp of American electoral politics. Zeus would descend from Mt. Olympus, mate with a sea nymph whose nectar had been spiked with the eye of an albino pelican, and Evan McMullin would spring forth from that union as President of the United States.

Many of the people who brought McMullin to political life were initially Rubio supporters. The thoroughly outlandish path to the presidency they had mapped out for McMullin was actually more fleshed out than the "Just add Florida!" plan they had for Rubio.

In the end, would-be President McMullin didn't even get half as many votes as Trump did in Utah, once again leaving many of the GOP's finest strategists standing outside in the cold, insulated by nothing more than their insistence that they were intellectually and morally superior to the people who kept handing their asses to them.

***

While 243 people in America were adding blue "M"s to their social media profile pictures to show that they were riding the McMullin wave, the more reality-based voters were digging in for what most thought would inevitably lead to Hillary Clinton becoming the second HISTORIC Democrat in a row to wreak havoc upon the Constitution.

I was still of the opinion that she would probably win, but I wasn't feeling an ass-kicking in the offing.

That Donald Trump had defied all the odds in his ascension to the Republican nomination should have been factored into pundits' predictions for November. For the most part, it wasn't.

Something else was happening that I was learning about, but not experiencing first hand. People were writing and telling stories about being outside of the coastal bubbles and encountering a lot of support for Trump.

They saw yard signs. They talked to people who were lifelong Democrats but were very quietly telling some that they were voting for Trump.

Kevin Downey Jr. is a good comedian friend of mine, and he was full of these stories. He and I first met several years ago when we were touring the South Pacific and doing shows for U.S. troops. Like me, Kevin is conservative but isn't a "conservative comic," meaning our acts aren't very political. Mine makes allusions to socio-political themes at times, but Kevin doesn't do any politics in his act, with one exception that I will explain in a moment.

Kevin likes to drive to gigs. He noticed that once he got out into small town America he would see a lot of Trump signs.

He was also polling audiences about their presidential preferences. This wasn't new for him, he had done it for previous elections and found that it was a pretty accurate barometer of the mood of the electorate.

Without having revealed any bias of his own (you really have to see Kevin's act to understand how true this is), he would ask who in the audience was voting for Hillary Clinton, then who was voting for Donald Trump.

The Trump response was so overwhelming that Kevin was the first person I knew personally to publicly state that the upset was in the making, and Hillary was going to lose. He told me he was fairly confident in the prediction but was "100% positive" that Trump would win by the time election day rolled around.

As we are in a business where 99 percent of our colleagues and friends are liberals, you can imagine the grief he was taking for this on social media.

Kevin has been enjoying one very long, glorious "I told you so" moment with them since.

Anecdotal evidence has always been easily dismissed, but it really was the drunk cousin no one wanted to acknowledge as far as the Big Data fetishists of 2016 were concerned.

Something was nagging at me though. All of the people who were supposed to know things about politics-myself included-had been proven to be wrong in so many ways by that point in the campaign that I found myself drawn to the inexact anecdotal evidence more and more.

Polls had been proven to be very wrong in previous elections too. Whenever that happened, the smart crowd would swear off believing in them, only to begin quoting polls for the next election about a month later.

I found myself in the enviable position of not being inclined to believe the people who had been wrong about everything.

Trump had huge rally crowds. Trump steamrolled a large, experienced Republican field in the primaries. Trump survived a variety of coup attempts before and during the Republican National Convention.

Hillary Clinton needed a rigged primary system to defeat the only Democrat who could inspire their base, and he wasn't even a real Democrat.

Those were the facts of the race in the fall of 2016. If one ignored the polls and examined only what I just presented, it was absurd to not even entertain the notion that Trump could win.

But...the polls!

The anecdotes kept pouring in, via social media and people I know around the country. The stories from outside the coastal bubbles were not at all similar to what the mainstream media was reporting.

People kept asking me what my gut feeling was. A lot of people. Relatives, friends, colleagues, and interviewers were hitting me up for predictions. I began each response by repeating my "I'm done making predictions," mantra.

While I had been wrong for most of the previous year and a half, I had still been through more presidential elections than almost everyone who was asking me questions. I knew I wasn't an idiot, it was just a weird election year. This realization helped me formulate a response to all of these queries that may not have been satisfying to everyone else, but that I felt confident in repeating.

I told everyone who asked that I truly believed that the Trump voters in middle America were being underrepresented in the polls and that we couldn't dismiss the fact that Hillary Clinton was one of the worse candidates in the history of presidential politics.

That was my way of saying that Trump could win without actually saying Trump could win, thus sticking to my promise of not making predictions.

I'm an American Roman Catholic, I rationalize very well.

The underrepresentation of the Trump voters could be explained by two things, although neither could be proven at the time.

First, confirmation bias in polling comes in varying degrees. Sometimes it is far more prevalent than usual.

Like when people truly want to believe an awful candidate is loved by the electorate.

That leads us to the second part.

Hillary Clinton's campaign was in a constant state of repackaging and re-introducing her to the voters. Her campaign floated 84 different slogans.[5]

Eighty four.

Her familiarity to the voters was supposed to be a selling point and they couldn't even zero in on one thing about her personality or resume that would stick.

While they kept flailing about for something that would resonate, they were being derisive about Trump's "Make America Great Again" slogan.

---

[5] https://www.nytimes.com/2016/11/10/us/politics/hillary-clinton-campaign.html

Hillary's career in politics was supposed to be the other pillar of her resume, but Trump's career as a businessman proved to give him a better grasp of branding. He didn't need eighty-plus trial balloons to see what would resonate with the public. While Team Hillary kept spit-balling to find a few words to make her palatable to the voting public Trump fans were snapping up red #MAGA hats as quickly as they could be made.

Any candidate who has been in the public eye for decades and still needs to be redefined by her campaign as the election draws nigh is redefining "problematic." Trump's headline-grabbing bombast worked out well for him as far as this glaring potential to fail of Hillary's was concerned. So many "smart" people were convinced that this would sink him. They never once closely examined the fact that Hillary Clinton's inability to connect with, well, humans after twenty-plus years of practice might be an overwhelming negative.

Far too much was read into the fact that Hillary was resonating with American celebrities. The Hollywood crowd's default position is to overwhelming support the Democrat in a presidential election.

Celebrities don't constitute a formidable voting bloc. If there were millions of them the story would be different. If that were the case, they wouldn't really be celebrities then, would they? Obviously, the disproportionate media access the celebs have makes it seem as if there are a lot of them.

They also aren't the magical get out the vote machine that many believe them to be. The people at the concerts for Hillary were already going to vote for her. No hearts and minds were changed. On election day, an American voter is still far more likely to be motivated to go to the polls and vote a certain way based on the state of his or her wallet than because Alec Baldwin hit some late-night shows and gushed about Hillary with the host like a couple of school girls.

The Democrats, bless their hearts, still truly believe that love from the Hollywood crowd is all they need. This was the party that as recently as the 2004 election was claiming to be the true champion of the working class in America.

Now they would have a difficult time telling you where the working class lived. To them, the map of the U.S. is now the Northeast, the West Coast, Hawaii, and "Icky Places."

***

As election day finally arrived, I was getting asked more and more for my thoughts on how it would go. I stuck to my non-prediction prediction and its two big caveats.

I wished I had gotten out and seen some firsthand evidence of the "roadside politics." I believed the people who were telling me about it but being in the belly of the California electoral beast made things like that difficult to truly grasp.

It was now time to see where this hottest of hot mess elections was going to end up.

Twelve

That's Why They Play the Game

Election Day 2016 was a beautiful, sunny affair in West Los Angeles, as most November days are there.

Despite having been through so many presidential elections, I never fail to be excited when it is time to go vote, even if I think my candidate is going to lose. We Americans are so privileged that, even after what we call "contentious" campaigns, our most important elections go off relatively smoothly. In many parts of the world, people still literally risk their lives to vote.

It is a right that I will always cherish, no matter how ridiculous the politics in this country get.

As I headed to my polling place a couple of blocks away, there was a little bounce in my step. No longer tethered to the two-headed major parties beast, I was feeling very good about my choice. That starkly contrasted to 2012, when I was most likely the most reluctant Romney voter in America1.

The calm was already upon me, I just hadn't gotten around to examining the reasons why.

I didn't have to walk very far because the line to vote practically ran back to my house. Smug, West Los Angeles liberals were chattering and taking pictures. They were saying "historic" over and over, as if they were being paid by the repetition.

It was Hillary Day in that line, and they were treating it as a holiday.

They were mostly older Democrats though. The Bernie Youth didn't seem to be turning out, at least in my neighborhood. There were plenty of them in the area too.

For the third election in a row, I was forced to fill out a provisional ballot because Los Angeles County had me listed as "permanent vote by mail" even though I had never once voted by mail or requested that I do it permanently. Also, every time I filled out a provisional ballot, I checked a box that requested I be removed from the vote by mail rolls. I despise early voting for a variety of reasons, and my registrar was trying to wear me down and get me to do it.

But voting irregularities don't exist, right?

After waiting in line with the Hillary Day celebrants I was forced to spend extra time there because I had to fill out my information for the provisional ballot. I may have been calm when I arrived, but the "festivities" going on around me were making me think of ways to shotgun a bottle of Jameson.

There was still writing and live-blogging to be done that afternoon, but I was going to be participating in a live broadcast that KABC radio was doing from a bar in the Valley that evening. I took a breath and paced myself.

As the television talking heads filled in the hours before the polls closed babbling just to hear themselves speak, I found myself paying no attention whatsoever to any of it. Well, I paid attention, because I had to, but I disregarded all of it. There are few things more useless than a political reporter speaking before the polls close. After the five thousand-month campaign, everything has been said. Other than the fashion choices of the electorate, there isn't anything to "report" about until election night.

They were all definitely dreamy-eyed at the thought of their concussed grandma cruising to an easy and, yes, HISTORIC, win though. They weren't trying to hide it either. The subtext to all of the "reporting" from the MSM was, "Today is the day we finally get rid of him!"

Hindsight isn't just 20/20, it's freakin' hilarious too.

I joined KABC's live broadcast after the polls had closed in the east and were almost closed in the Midwest. The bar was packed with mostly conservative listeners who most definitely weren't Hillary supporters and they seemed very loose and happy.

In Los Angeles County.

That was quite different from my West Side experience earlier in the day.

On air, I gave my patented non-prediction with the now almost worn out caveats. I was paired with a Democratic strategist who was a veteran of the Clinton White House. She was cautiously optimistic, but not in full gloat mode like the media people were.

When we got around to talking about messaging I said that I thought Hillary's only real message in the closing months was, "I'm not him." The strategist didn't disagree with me.

By the time I got off the air, the media people were just beginning to get the first notes of panic in their voices regarding Pennsylvania. It was a truly delicious sound, one I wish I'd recorded for posterity.

Having no real skin in the game, I was able to view what played out in the next few hours with detached amusement. It was as if I were watching a Netflix original movie about all the news media types I loathed, written by someone I agreed with politically. What I was about to experience some of the best televised entertainment I had seen in years.

While I was mingling with some of the radio people in the bar we got word that one of the few Trump-friendly contributors on CNN (a friend and colleague) just had his one scheduled hit that night changed to three. The original was probably just thought to be a post-mortem recap, but something was now afoot.

Pennsylvania had already been called by a few news outlets by the time I was getting a ride home (there was drinking involved). If it was all going to blow up in Hillary's face I wanted to enjoy it from the comfort of my own home, not in the damn Valley. I followed everything on Twitter (like a normal person) on the ride back.

By the time I had settled on my couch and turned the television on, Trump had probably won the election. The mainstream media were struggling to report that, however. You could see it in their sad puppy eyes, but the words of truth just wouldn't come.

They couldn't really be blamed for this, as truth wasn't something they were ever allowed to flirt with as Hillary advocates. After years of reflexively spewing propaganda about a woman even they probably couldn't stand, they were so far from the truth about anything they would need Sherpa guides to get them back to it.

The electoral map, however, was turning redder by the minute, and denial wasn't going to work long as an editorial strategy.

When they all finally had to report that, yes, Donald J. Trump was going to be the next President of the United States, my real entertainment began. I finally got tired of flipping between CNN and MSNBC to watch the anguish unfold in real time, so I kept one on my television and streamed one on my phone. I would bounce back and forth with the audio, but I could see all of the faces cycling between horror, grief, and bewilderment and it was riveting.

This *Cirque du Sadness* went on for the next several hours, and I could not pull myself away. The members of the American mainstream media were now exposing their bias with their expressions, and not just with their words. MSNBC's Rachel Maddow was particularly overwrought, and therefore one of the most fun to watch well into the wee hours. Maddow's bewildered angst would occasionally be broken up by Katy Tur, the NBC News reporter who had covered the Trump campaign. Each time Tur weighed in, she looked like a four-year-old kid who had just been told on Christmas Eve that there was no Santa Claus. All she could do was repeat the MSM reasons for not voting for Trump, obviously annoyed that the American electorate didn't listen to her.

I didn't know it was possible to get that much pleasure from watching a guy I didn't even vote for win an election. Had it merely been about Trump defeating Hillary, it most likely wouldn't have held as much entertainment value. He'd just crushed the spirits of the thoroughly biased and dishonest American political press. I had been writing about liberal media bias for over a decade and a half by then and the MSM's comeuppance on November 8th, 2016 was pure delight for me.

The icing on the cake was the fact that Granny couldn't even make it to the podium for a concession speech. In the media's darkest hour, the woman they'd just spent two years telling us should be our leader didn't have the courage or strength to offer words of support for those who had given all for her, probably because she was face-down in a chardonnay bath.

Their defeat was made more complete by that.

The Trump presidency was yet to come and there was no way to know what that would hold, but his election night brought me waves of enjoyment that I could never have anticipated.

That would do for the moment.

Thirteen

Russian to Conclusions

The United States of America, having just emerged from the strangest of presidential campaigns and topping it off with a surprise ending on election night, may have thought the weirdness was over.

However, the lead-up to the post-election madness was quaint and quirky compared to the generous helpings of utter batshit that American liberals were about to start heaping on the national political conversation.

Doing their best to make the United States look like some backwater dictatorship that had just experienced a sham election, liberals were in the throes of a visceral denial that, for a while, looked like they might be willing to burn it all down just to prove how mad they were that they didn't get their way.

They did the one thing that leftists do well-they marched in protest. Lord, do these people know how to show up out of the ether like the Children of the Corn to suddenly form a throng of angry marchers. The problem with these leftist mobs is that they never really want anything more than to let everyone know that they are mad.

Yeah, we got that.

A most hilarious piece of information immediately emerged from these post-election protests: a lot of the diaper-wetting kids who were flooding the streets in anger didn't even vote for Hillary.[6] They voted for the Green Party, they wrote in

---

[6] https://www.washingtonpost.com/news/post-nation/wp/2016/11/16/anti-

Bernie, or they stayed home and ate Taco Bell after getting stoned. They were too stupid to know that they were really mad at themselves.

This was around the time that I began adopting my, "it's all a circus and I'm going to enjoy watching" attitude.

It may seem cold-hearted to some, but I thoroughly enjoyed every tear-filled moment these idiots experienced. I couldn't muster any sympathy for people who were that hysterical over the result of an election in the freest country on Earth, where they were guaranteed to have another shot at getting what they wanted.

When Barack Obama was elected in 2008, I was, to no one's surprise, exceedingly unhappy with the result. He was a progressive whose talk of "fundamental transformation" made conservatives like me very nervous.

There was also the fact that I had put in a lot of effort to help John McCain get elected. He wasn't my ideal candidate at the time, but I was still in "he's less awful than the Democrat" mode.

It was clear very early how things were going to go on election night in '08, so my then ten-year-old daughter and I headed out to our favorite Italian restaurant up the street.

There may have been some wine involved but I didn't want to sit around moping. My daughter knew that I'd done a lot to try and help McCain win, and as we were walking home she asked me if I was sad. I told her (quite honestly) that I wasn't. She looked at me a bit skeptically and mentioned that I'd really wanted McCain to win.

What I said to her next I believed then and still do now.

"I'm not sad because this is America, and we'll have another one of these elections in four years. If my candidate doesn't win all I can do is wake up the next day and be ready to fight for the next candidate."

I remember being a bit crestfallen the first time my candidate didn't win, which was 1992 (when the successful Clinton won). I'd been 3-0 out of the gate in presidential elections though, so it was just weird. I certainly didn't feel compelled to march and scream.

And I think people who do are idiots, which is why I take such delight in their anguish. Idiots should suffer. In fact, if I ever do run for office, my entire platform may be promising to make idiots suffer again.

MISA

I'll have to see how that looks on a hat.

Nah, too reminiscent of Jar-Jar Binks.

***

Just when I thought the kids might cry themselves to sleep and let the rest of us enjoy the American tradition of a peaceful transition of power, the biggest nothingburger in the history of Unites States politics was being cooked up by the Democratic brain trust and their flying media monkeys.

American liberals – long suspect in the reality participation department – decided to give up the ghost of pretense and offer incontrovertible proof that Hillary Clinton's loss to Donald Trump had pushed them to the brink of a psychotic break: for the first time since the Cuban Missile Crisis, they were worried that Russia may be a dangerous threat to our way of life.

After 54 years, the Big Red Bear was a threat again to the other side.

I grew up during the tail end of the Cold War. Democrats, progressives and other American lefties were largely Soviet apologists back then. It was a lot of the same crap you hear from them today about North Korea, Cuba, or any other commie hellhole starves its own people. As long as a regime can whip up a quick Potemkin Village tour for a low-functioning American celebrity who then comes back to the U.S. and sings its praises, the left never fails to fall in love with communists.

Had the American voting public ever been wholly enthralled and swayed by the political opinions of Hollywood types, this country would have been flushed down the communist toilet long ago.

Thankfully, a lot of us are still not listening to them.

Those of us who can reference history that goes back more than a month or so remember President Obama's line from the 2012 campaign mocking Mitt Romney for saying that Russia was "our No.1 geopolitical foe" and celebrating The Lightbringer's dismissiveness of that idea.[7]

In four short years, Russia had gone from being a laughable threat to the monster under the bed, in the closet, and in the voting booth in the American liberal fever dream.

The subtext of all of this is even more stunning. As they wildly flailed about to find excuses for Hillary Clinton having lost the election, they ended up with one in which they were essentially admitting that Barack Obama was a paste-eating idiot when it came to foreign policy.

---

[7]

https://www.salon.com/2012/10/23/obama_the_80s_called_they_want_their_foreign_policy_back/

They didn't (and still don't) realize they were doing this, of course. In their minds, Obama is a messianic figure whose every breath is divine and a man who can do no wrong. That breath of his that included the zinger that they all celebrated in 2012 has been all but erased from their hive mind.

Still, their sheer panic from the realization that the pop star/late night show host one-two punch wasn't enough to elect a president essentially forced them to throw their messiah under the bus.

My response: "What's not to enjoy here?"

The severing of a longtime party affiliation was my first step in political emotional freedom, but it was the newfound Russia fetish of the American liberals that really gave me wings. It was impossible for me to watch that unfold without taking delight in the absurdity of it all.

The early days of the Soviet Union were presided over by a Russian mass murderer who deliberately starved millions of his own people.

American liberal elites loved Russia then.

For most of the post-Stalin Soviet Union's history, the citizens were severely neglected in order to facilitate a military build-up designed solely to destroy the West, specifically the United States.

American liberal elites loved Russia then.

Post-Soviet Union, a former Soviet strongman emerged as Russia's leader and made no effort to conceal his less-than-delicate ambitions. Russia invaded Georgia and the Ukraine, all the while strengthening its ties with Iran.

American liberal elites laughed off Russia as a threat then.

A candidate with the combined people skills of Jeffrey Dahmer and a high school bully lost a presidential election that Beyoncé and Jay-Z told everyone she should win.

American liberal elites decided Russia is the devil.

That's what it took to change their minds.

If I were a better person, I might have felt badly for them. Thankfully, I am bound by no such constraints. Their tortured fixation on a newly minted bogey man to explain away Hillary Clinton's personality and campaign strategy flaws was the greatest theater in America at the time.

That they all actually thought it might turn into an immediate reversal of the election results and magically install Hillary in the Oval Office just made me feel as if I had VIP seats.

Adding layers of deliciousness to my experience was the fact that I was surrounded by liberals. Finally, that had become a plus. Every time one of them expressed worry about the Russians I would reply by saying that it was nice to see so many people on the left coming around to the conservative position on them.

They wouldn't cry, but I could tell they wanted to.

While I am still uncertain exactly how to pronounce schadenfreude because German is stupid and I'm glad we won World War II and don't have to speak it, I knew then I was experiencing so much of it I might develop an addiction.

Had I voted for Trump I may not have been as able to enjoy the transition period madness. I probably would have been too worried about how he'd govern to just give in and let the spectacle wash over me. I had no trepidation about what he or the Republicans would do after the inauguration because they weren't my people anymore. Add to that the fact that nobody in Washington had been doing anything I'd wanted for a couple of decades and I was enjoying a remarkably pleasant, expectation-free existence.

I was essentially applying my approach to watching action movies to the American political dramatics of late 2016 and early 2017.

Action flicks are my favorite kind of movie. Most comedies now aren't funny. Too many dramas are preachy and they have feelings, which I abhor.

A good action movie is a ballet of explosions, gun fire, and car chases. Feelings are kept to minimum, if they exist at all. For example, I think "G.I. Joe: The Rise of Cobra" may be the greatest movie I've ever seen. It wastes no time before things get blown up, it has hot women fighting, and ninjas.

Yes, ninjas.

With those elements in place, who cares if the acting is one-dimensional or the dialog sucks?

I reiterate: hot women fighting, and ninjas.

Minimum expectation, maximum enjoyment. That's where I was in November and December of 2016.

There may not have been any ninjas, and you're certainly not going to find any hot women in a frothing leftist protest horde, but the ever-increasing emotional explosions were quite satisfying to me.

The Democrats were finally afraid of Russia, and it was only because they had a masochistic desire to spend at least four years being scolded by a power-mad drunk grandma who dressed like Chairman Mao.

A woman they had unceremoniously rejected for the same job eight years earlier.

If I had any coding skills I would turn that hot mess into a video game just so I could relive the fun for years to come.

***

The immediate post-election madness from the seething anti-Trump people was so full of "hold my beer" moments that I feared we might run out of beer. I love beer, so that truly was my only real worry.

As 2016 was about to yield to 2017 I finally realized that these adult toddlers had some serious lungs on them and weren't going to stop wailing in their ideological corner any time soon. Thankfully, they weren't also soiling themselves in the process.

As far as I could tell, anyway.

The political picture in America was having a sort of emotional Dorian Gray effect on me by this point. The angrier that the anti-Trump left and the Never Trump right got, the calmer and more amused I became.

I was binge-watching American politics, and I was having a lot of fun. Unlike binge-watching a show on Netflix or Amazon, however, I wasn't going to be running out of episodes anytime soon.

The reason for this became clear to me in a rare epiphany.

Thanks to Trump's victory, American liberals were actually in their element. Liberals love to be angry. It's their default mode. The more progressive that the American left has become, the angrier it's gotten. They're mad at successful people. They're mad that there really are two genders. It's pretty easy to see that most of them are mad at mommy and/or daddy.

It's what they do.

The election of Donald Trump enabled American leftists to take their everyday anger and whip it into an orgiastic frenzy. He had created a feedback loop of anger for them that was making their lives exactly what they wanted them to be. No longer did they have to cast about each day for something to focus their inherent anger upon-Trump was already there when they woke up and not going away. What Trump's mere existence didn't directly provide to the daily progressive anger cycle, the cognitive dissonance they must have felt because, deep down, they knew he was perfect for their rage needs, made up for. He was doing everything for them and doing it for free.

It was a liberal's dream scenario.

As I prepared for what would end up being the crappiest year of my life, little did I know how much the misery of the American left would function as a soothing balm for my own.

Part Three: To the Presidency and Beyond!

Fourteen

Yes, He's Your President

On Inauguration Day 2017, I began a new editing gig for a political site that, for the most part, I hated (the gig and the site, that it). I had to do many things that were anathema to me like work with other people, wake up early, and read email.

It was to be a partnering even more doomed than a relationship between two people who announce their status on Facebook and keep telling everyone how happy they are.

The job did, however, give me the chance to head back to Arlington, VA for a couple of weeks in February to see some of the political drama in person, and do it from the belly of the beast. Well, I was belly-adjacent in Arlington.

Another layer of deliciousness.

The site was really right-leaning but was going through some growing pains and employed quite a few twenty-somethings who fancied themselves enlightened liberal journalists.

It wasn't too difficult to figure out who in the sprawling office was #WithHer and still reeling from the thought that Donald Trump was now indeed the President of the United States. Their pained smiles as they pretended to go along with the right-wing flow delighted me to now end. For that brief period in time, working around other people wasn't so bad.

In the middle of the trip I headed to New York to make what would be my last appearance on the Fox News Channel show "Red Eye" before it was canceled (obviously, I didn't know it would be the last at the time).

The show, for those of you unfamiliar with it, was a topical panel show that featured a weird mix of Fox News personalities, musicians, comedians, actors and other political types. Fox News aired it at 3 AM Eastern and never gave it any promo. It was psychotic fun. I was a fan before I was a guest. I remember seeing it the very first week it aired in 2007 and enjoying the dark, biting takes on the news of the day. It was as if me and my conservative friends were sitting around drinking and mocking what was considered newsworthy that day.

It was perfect for me. Took me two years to finally get on, but it happened.

"Red Eye" lasted for ten years, largely because it pulled in better numbers in the middle of the night than CNN's prime time shows. It had a loyal cult following and I wish it were still around. Cable news is mostly televised constipation. I've never liked it very much, and it just continues to get worse.

That's probably best left for another time.

I left for New York from Washington one month after Trump had been inaugurated. Four weeks in and CNN alone had already done about 17,000 unhinged things in the name of journalism. The next night's taping was guaranteed to be fun.

The anti-Trump fare that not-so-fine (the weather is always awful on the east coast in the winter) February day that we were to cover on the show was a hodgepodge of inanity that was, of course, quite serious to those peddling it.

One story involved an interpreter who freelanced for several American broadcast networks analyzing Trump's speech patterns.[8] Naturally, he was not a fan.

My personal favorite was a lengthy Twitter rant by the person running Sweden's official account. He took umbrage

---

[8] https://www.mediaite.com/online/interpreters-say-theyre-vexed-by-trumpese-if-we-translated-trump-verbatim-we-would-sound-stupid/

with the fact that President Trump said Sweden was experiencing problems with the migrant and immigrant populations in the country.[9] Much to what I'm sure was the chagrin of all involved in the official Swedish Twitter Department, riots broke out in a largely immigrant part of Stockholm not long after the rant.[10]

Oops.

The story we covered that was most representative of the adolescent churlishness being exhibited by the anti-Trump people on a daily basis involved a grocery story that carried the Trump wine brand.[11]

The adult children in the "hate Trump" camp, spurred on by the sweet gals over at the National Organization for Women, were trying to organize a boycott of an entire grocery chain over one brand on its shelves.

Grown up, no?

For the record, I've always thought boycotts were stupid. My position on that may be evolving a bit, but I'm still largely of the mind that they're group tantrums that feel a bit too much like mob rule, especially when organized by leftists, who are inherently hate-based. I've eschewed them even when called for by people who I agree with against corporations I that feel are deserving of derision.

Deride, don't boycott.

My comments on the incident that night on the show would end up being something that I repeat variations of to

---

[9] https://theweek.com/speedreads/681347/person-running-swedens-twitter-account-massive-antitrump-rant

[10] https://hotair.com/archives/2017/02/21/perfect-timing-sweden-copes-with-riot-in-mostly-immigrant-suburb-of-stockholm/

[11] http://www.foxnews.com/food-drink/2017/02/20/wegmans-supermarket-sells-out-trump-wine-after-proposed-boycott.html

this day. I mentioned that I hadn't even voted for Trump and, for the most part, was just a casual observer. However, every day since he'd been in office it felt like the Trump haters were bringing a bulldozer up behind me and pushing me towards liking him because they were being so ridiculous. At the rate they were going, I said I might end up phone-banking for him by the summer.

That is the thing about the modern American progressive penchant for mob rule: it's not winning any hearts and minds. Then again, they don't really want to. They want to publicly shame corporations and individuals into bending to their will. That's quite ironic coming from the very same people who have been waging so many anti-bullying crusades in recent years. Bullying is all these emotional midgets have.

A frenzied mob may be able to scare some people into joining it, but members of civilized society aren't inclined to embrace frothing hordes. They're more inclined to be pushed away by that behavior and towards the very thing upon which the horde is focusing its rage.

Do bear in mind here that if I am on the side of "civilized" society something has gone horribly, horribly awry.

Great job lefties, you've almost normalized me. That's not going to make me more sympathetic to your cause.

I hate normal.

***

I arrived back in the DC area the next night, which was the unofficial kickoff for the Conservative Political Action Conference. CPAC is the largest annual gathering of people who think they're conservatives (at least half who attend really aren't) in America. I am not a regular CPAC-goer, as so many of my friends are. I had only been twice before, and the last time had been six years earlier.

This particular version was one I was looking forward to, however, because I wanted to see how the MAGA and Never Trump crowds were going to mingle.

As Chauncey Gardiner said in "Being There": I like to watch.

Thousands of people who had been exchanging a lot of social media enmity for months were now going to be thrown together in one big-ass hotel and drinking a lot (political people are miserable, there is always an excessive amount of drinking-it's the most bipartisan thing happening in Washington).

Naturally, I was hoping for the worst, just for my personal amusement. I didn't want riots – that's too leftist – but a nice big lobby brawl where the participants were permanently banned from the conference would have been fun to see.

Alas, there was enough booze to make everyone too mellow to care about the grievances of the previous several months. Sure, there were one or two contentious discussions, but no arrests. It's not fun until someone gets arrested.

Things between the two camps have since deteriorated more, but I will get to that later.

The other draw for me at the 2017 conference was the fact that President Trump was scheduled to speak. I've met a lot of politicians in my activist life but had never been anywhere near the President of the United States. And while I may be a contentious partisan, I am also a patriot. I would think it an honor to see or meet the president, no matter the party affiliation.

Thanks to the new gig, I had media/press credentials and, yes, that made me feel creepy. But they were my ticket to Trump's speech on Friday morning.

The room was huge and I was in back with the media people I'd spent years loathing. At least I had two conservative friends with me who also had credentials.

The nonsense about Trump trying to disenfranchise the press was already in full swing after his first month in office. Half of the massive room was media. If he was trying to shut them up, he was failing.

No, I wasn't expecting a sudden bout of self-awareness to hit the eternally clueless American political press corps. However, had it not been so early in the morning (for me, that's anything before noon) I may have pointed out how wrong they were to some of them but I was running on just one cup of coffee that, to my horror, didn't have any whiskey in it.

Not surprisingly, very few of the Never Trump conservative media types showed up. I can't really remember any being there but, again, it was a large room. I do remember afterwards though, when many of them were acting as if not showing up had earned them some sort of purity merit badge, much like they thought their miserably failed McMullen votes did.

The stark contrast in the two halves of the room was fun. The front half was loaded with people who were thrilled to be there for the chance to see a president they most overwhelmingly supported. There was more buzzing and smiling than I thought possible for the morning.

Maybe their coffee did have whiskey.

The media people in the back half generally had frustrated, dour looks on their faces. It was understandable. Most of them spend the majority of their time operating in a bubble that doesn't expose them to people who have different political leanings than they do. Being exposed to a large group of people who they generally pretend don't exist must have overwhelming for the poor dears.

The more I examined them, the happier I was that I had the creepy media pass and could witness this angst up close.

My friends and I decided to make it clear early on that we weren't that kind of "media." Before the president even arrived, we were taking selfies, laughing, and enjoying being Americans.

The others were not amused, especially by the "enjoying being Americans" part. Liberals hate anyone who doesn't want to be French or Swedish.

Which merely inspired us to keep doing it, of course.

When President Trump made his entrance, we cheered along with the non-media types in the front. I was doing it to be antagonistic, and it worked. A quick glance at the faces around me told me that I wouldn't be having cocktails with any of my "fellow media" colleagues soon.

As he began to speak after the crowd finally settled down (that took some time), I saw a completely different Trump than I ever had before. Admittedly, I didn't pay much attention to his rallies during the campaign. Sure, I would see a quick clip or two, but I never watched more than a few seconds of one.

I had seen his contentious moments when dealing directly with the media, however, and thought we might be in for more of the same, even though he wouldn't be interacting with them that day.

Trump in his element in front of a friendly crowd of supporters is a very different thing to behold. He is relaxed almost to the point where you think he might request that a chair be brought on stage so he can sit down and turn it into a sort of fireside chat.

He still rambles a bit, but I have never faulted him for that. I've been speaking for a living for over thirty years and I often ramble when speaking to a crowd, even if I'm working from an outline.

His rambling is a nitpicky point that only bothers his detractors anyway. Unlike his predecessor – who was a train wreck without one – Trump doesn't like to work from a teleprompter and things can meander a bit. You just kind of get into the rhythm of it.

One thing I did know was that Trump is very adept at giving red meat to his supporters during speeches. He throws it out there like he's feeding lions at the circus. Most politicians who have real success do this. The difference with Trump, though, is that he has a knack for finding the red meat that will not only fire up his troops but maximize the amount of offense it gives his haters. His complete lack of filter or regard for political correctness both aid him greatly in doing this.

To be sure, President Obama used to say things that I found offensive quite often. That's one reason that I only paid attention to his speeches if I was being paid to comment on them later. He didn't push my buttons the way President Trump pushes the media's though. He has a singular gift for making the press corps want to inhale Xanax and wash it down with whatever craft cocktail the New York Times told them to be obsessed with that week (all of the left media take their cues from the New York Times).

Content-wise, I found nothing objectionable in the speech. It was probably the first time I had ever paid attention to the substance of a Trump speech (other than his acceptance speech at the RNC, which was a slightly different animal) beyond the barbs he throws at the media.

I could have easily voted for the president I was seeing that day.

His performance didn't exactly make me Team MAGA, but it did validate my contention that his mere presence in the Oval Office didn't pose a threat to the future of the United States, which is what my Never Trump friends at the conference were still insisting.

As the speech ended I realized that I had found the entire thing entertaining. That was happening a lot by that point. The over the top anguish of the media, the still-stunned look in the eyes of the Purity Merit Badge Never Trump crowd, and now the tangential wit of the president -- it was all one big production that was providing almost nonstop entertainment for me.

I'm not even a guy who likes to enjoy things very much. Comedians by nature are usually dark and brooding. Sure, I fake it well, but I'm 50 shades of pitch black dark night of the soul on the inside (I know that doesn't make much sense, but work with me here). It's better for joke writing. Jerry Seinfeld is the only happy person in modern stand-up who is funny.

My unfamiliarity with being relaxed and enjoying things made it difficult for me to identify exactly what these things were as they were happening. That was also balanced out by the new gig and all of that waking up early crap. It distracted me from the lighter hearted stuff. I would notice little things like how much I enjoyed the speech, but I was in the midst of an evolving political worldview that was going to be in need of the hindsight treatment I'm giving it now.

***

The title of this chapter alludes to a personal pet peeve of mine. I don't know when people began doing this, maybe it's an attitude that has been around since the days of John Adams.

People who didn't vote for the particular president in office are fond of saying "He's not my president."

With President Trump, there is the double-whammy of both Democrats and some Never Trump types saying that.

Conservatives used to do this when President Obama was in office. It was irritating then too. I would roundly criticize them for doing so.

Many people justify this infantile nonsense by convincing themselves that any election their candidate loses was "stolen." Some conservatives would make that claim to me after Mitt Romney *handed* an election to Barack Obama and I would just laugh at them. I could buy a goldfish to run against Romney and it would win four out of five elections.

Some of the disgruntlement among Democrats in 2016-2017 stemmed from Hillary's win in the popular vote, most of which was due to California. Her overwhelming margin there had as much to do with shifting demographics as it did with the fact that a lot of Republicans in the Golden State have just given up. It's unlikely that you will find a more moribund political party in any other state. If George Romero were still alive he would be working on a movie about the California GOP called "Vote of the Living Dead" to complete his series of zombie masterpieces.

Democrats hate the Electoral College because they want New York and California to be able to elect every president.

Either way, Obama's victory in 2012 was legit, as was Trump's in 2016. People who say otherwise need some sort of mental health supervision.

Just growing up a little would help too.

Once more, this is me saying this, people.

We're doomed.

Fifteen

The Virtue Lotion Massage

It is the spring of 2018 as I write this and there is no point in even mentioning what the Trump administration turmoil *du jour* is because it may very well change before I finish typing a sentence about it. Such is the nature of politics in the contentious Trump vs Mainstream Media era.

There is no doubt that the president himself is the catalyst for much of the turmoil. As I well know, being a no-filter person means that one's lack of inner censor can lead to frequent public awkwardness. The lack of filter works well for me on stage but when I am forced into polite society I often wish that I had a voice inside my head that would at least whisper, "Shut up," every once in a while.

In the private sector, President Trump's shoot-from-the-lip style probably wasn't a liability. He was, after all, the head of the company. People put up with all sorts of peccadilloes from the boss when they're being well paid or trying to move up the corporate ladder.

While he may have been used to a lot of publicity, Trump wasn't used to having his every moment in public chronicled. I feel for the guy. If people were recording me all day there would be a public movement afoot to have me institutionalized. Suffice it to say that a fair amount of the hot water the president finds himself in he has boiled on his own.

Having conceded that, let us move on to the subject of this chapter: the thorough, undeniable, smelly-sock awfulness of the American mainstream media.

I was going to qualify that as "political media" but, in reality, most of the MSM is political. When I rail against the mainstream media (which is quite frequently) people on the left will counter with a pathetically nonsensical argument which posits that the cable news ratings domination of the Fox News Channel and talk radio negate any claims of liberal media bias.

Yeah...about that.

Cable news and talk radio are watched and listened to almost exclusively in echo chambers. The only liberals watching Fox News are the people being paid to monitor and criticize it. The three major cable news networks all have a decided bias. CNN is rather new to the game, having spent a long time trying to be somewhat centrist. The two problems it faced were that centrist doesn't sell on cable, and it was always run by liberals, who don't know what centrist looks like.

The network news broadcasts are still where the great white whale of American politics – the undecided voter – are getting their information. My mom watches the evening news. Your cousins who only pay attention to politics three months before an election watch the evening news. Despite the fact that we are wrapping up the second decade of the 21st Century, a lot of people still do things the old fashioned way.

Network news viewership dwarfs cable news. A dominating night for one of the primetime cable hosts will see numbers between 2 and 3 ½ million,[12] while the lowest performing network news broadcast can double or triple that.[13]

And guess what kids? ABC, NBC, and CBS are all biased for the left.

Your Aunt Cindy in Cedar Rapids is getting most of her information about President Trump from anchors who are de facto spokespersons for the Democratic National Committee.

That's why she drinks. Oh, Aunt Cindy.

I would go into detail justifying that claim (the spokespersons thing, not the Aunt Cindy is a drunk thing – everyone knows she it) but many fine books have already been written on the subject and I have been addressing it in various forums for years. Google must have some of my work on it available for perusal.

NBC is the worst of the Big Three. The NBC News division is the mothership for MSNBC, so this isn't even up for discussion. Anyone who thinks there is an ideological difference between the broadcast news people and the "Che" t-shirt-wearing Cheerleader Squad at MSNBC is concussed.

---

[12] ,https://www.forbes.com/sites/markjoyella/2018/03/02/msnbc-beats-fox-news-as-rachel-maddow-has-one-of-tvs-top-shows-thursday/
[13] http://www.adweek.com/tvnewser/evening-news-ratings-week-of-april-2-3/361454

NBC News also gave us Brian Williams and Matt Lauer, who were two of their most prominent on-air personalities for years. A pathological liar and a serial sex abuser.

Almost eight million Americans watch their news coverage every weeknight.

The "Fox News dominance balances out the bias" conversation is over before it starts, really. Bill O'Reilly at his peak still wasn't getting as many viewers as the third-rated network news anchor, who I wouldn't be able to name without looking it up.

CNN may have been looking up for a very long time at Fox News in the official ratings but it is still the network that is on almost every television in every large airport in America. What it lacks in voluntary viewership it more than makes up for with its captive audience.

Obviously, not everyone in the airport is paying attention to CNN. It's powerful branding, however, and creates the illusion that CNN is the network for regular Americans.

The network news anchors and journalists will all swear that they are objective and unbiased.

They are all lying. Worse yet, they know they are lying.

Years ago, I would have believed that some people at NBC News truly believed they were true journalists who had a lot of integrity. They still would have been wrong, but I would at least have conceded that they believed it.

Journalistic objectivity in America was under assault for decades. It received a mortal wound in 2016. As the Trump-hating press became more interested in acting out because they're feelings were hurt by the election, that wound became even more grave. By the end of President Trump's first year in office, it had been dead so long that it was a putrid, rotting husk.

***

Talk radio has long been a sore spot for media leftists because it is the one broadcast medium in which they haven't been able to marginalize center-right and/or conservative voices.

Conservative talk radio grew out of the overwhelming need for non-liberals in America to have a place to vent. We were essentially exiled to a broadcast island where we could all spend a few hours saying, "Yeah, that really sucks."

Talk radio doesn't win any hearts and minds though. No one casually happens upon the Rush Limbaugh show and thinks, "Hey, who's this guy? I'll give him a listen." Successful talk radio hosts get that way by being firebrands. They aren't there to make friends, they're around to give an extremely partisan audience something to get fired up about that day. It's destination listening, if you will.

This is even more true in the era of satellite radio. Gone are the days when people drove around and were limited to whatever radio stations had strong signals wherever they happened to be at the time. I can't remember the last time I was in a car and somebody just perused the radio "dial" to see what was available.

The biggest reason that talk radio is destination radio is that the bias isn't something that is shied away from. It's a feature, not a bug. That's why it's called *conservative* talk radio. A guy who sleeps in hemp boxers and douses himself with patchouli upon arising isn't going to accidentally hear Sean Hannity's radio show and listen for a while as he tends to his plot at the community garden.

While individual conservative radio personalities still dominate the market for the most part, taxpayer-funded and unabashedly liberal NPR sits atop the ratings as I write this.[14] That means that we can now put to rest the assertion that talk radio somehow magically cancels out liberal media bias.

***

The media bias I speak of extends far beyond news broadcasts. The entertainment industry is dominated by liberals. This isn't a secret, they brag about it. It was lorded over us in 2016 as a weapon of mass political destruction that we couldn't hope to combat. The fact that Donald Trump prevailed isn't exactly a one-off event, but it is a rare victory.

American celebrity liberals are secular evangelists, especially now. Their politics are religion to them and they never miss a chance to proselytize. An irritating combination of 16th Century missionary, Amway salesperson, and someone who doesn't read nearly as much as he or she thinks he or she does, entertainment industry liberals politicize everything.

While there is certainly a place in art and entertainment for political expression there is also a lot to be said for both being modes of escape rather than wallowing in the political problems of the day. Even Bob Dylan takes a break to write songs about women, love and sex every once in a while.

Political statements are now a part of even what should be the most benign, escapist entertainment. This goes largely unnoticed by left-leaning consumers of the Hollywood product because they're so used to political statements being interjected into every conversation that it's like living near a

---

[14] https://www.npr.org/about-npr/597590072/npr-maintains-highest-ratings-ever

train track and not having the noise register once you get used to it. (I know whence I speak-I just moved into a house near the tracks a month ago. The train noise was grating for the first couple of weeks, then it became comforting background noise.)

If you are a center-right or conservative consumer of entertainment, it often becomes cringe-worthy if you can't compartmentalize.

A 30-minute network sitcom features about 22 minutes of non-commercial time. In those 22 minutes it is not unusual to hear at least three Democratic and/or progressive talking points shoehorned into the dialogue just for the sake of having them there and letting the other lefties know that all involved in the production are on board with the agenda.

Scratch that. Almost all are on board. There are many behind the camera people in the industry who aren't liberal. They have to remain closeted for fear of losing their jobs.

For the most part, however, the money people and the major players are marching in lock-step with the lefty crusade.

Network dramas are even worse. They may as well spend half of each episode with the lead actors in a pulpit. Conservatives are bludgeoned by dialogue that sounds as if it were written by political speechwriters rather than professional television people.

This was all happening before Trump was elected. It's become an artistic cancer since he's been in office.

The larger point here is that the continual preaching of leftist dogma on network television is where media bias transforms from a news outlet annoyance for conservatives into a mainstream monster on steroids. The entertainment programming reach versus news programming is overwhelming.

Mainstream televised entertainment is one huge leftist indoctrination factory. Americans who aren't particularly inclined to one political party or another are exposed to a bombardment of liberal orthodoxy every time they turn on the TV. More importantly, their kids are being exposed to it. We may be in a Golden Age of television as far as the small screen artistry being created on the cable networks, but the networks have elevated propaganda to an art form that old commie regimes would drool over.

The lines between network news and network entertainment have been blurring for a very long time. In the Trump era, however, the entities have begun working with incestuous synergy, all of it borne of hatred for the President of the United States.

***

As the first several months of Trump's presidency wore on I began to notice a new camaraderie being forged among members of the mainstream media.

While I don't watch a lot of cable news (practically none, actually), I do spend a good part of each day monitoring the Twitter interactions of the major players at FNC, CNN, and MSNBC. When I'm not writing jokes, I'm blogging about politics and I have to pay attention to the news and the people who make it and report it. I should have developed an ulcer if I were playing by Trump era rules. People I've known for years who used to be rational and not easily ruffled have become hand-wringing ninnies whose moods are dictated by the whims of the 24-hour news cycle.

I searched my brain for a word that was in regular use after the 1920s but "ninnies" still seemed the most apropos.

As each day of Trump's presidency passed in early 2017 and the Magic Election Reversal Fairy didn't show up, the MSM began synchronized a freak out that manifested itself as a daily smirking and back-patting party, the purpose of which was to reassure each other that the 2016 election didn't mean that their mojo was completely lost.

Face it, until Trump won in 2016, they'd had a pretty good eight year run selling the Democratic party line to the American public. If they met with any resistance they simply barked "Racism!" and went back to penning love haiku to Barack Obama. For the journos in their 20s and early 30s, this was the bulk of their careers. To them, journalism meant sticking to a politically correct leftist script that all their friends agreed with and never meeting any resistance for doing so.

That sort of made them the cool kids in their own minds while Obama was president. With this skewed perspective it's easy to see why they thought that Hillary would be an easy sell despite the fact that even the people who like her don't like her. They figured that any detractors could be silenced by simply calling them sexists. Most will admit that it never entered their minds that Donald Trump could win the election. They were looking forward to another eight years of eating lunch at one of the good tables in the high school cafeteria.

Trump waltzed through the cafeteria in 2016, grabbed their lunch trays, shoved mash potatoes in their smug faces, and told them to move.

To another school.

They were shaken, embarrassed and feeling bullied. Liberals think anyone who points out their obvious weaknesses and/or flaws is bullying them. Reality is the biggest bully of all to the Participation Trophy Era people.

The self-preservation instinct can be strong even in the most emotionally weak among us. The ranks of the liberal mainstream media in America are filled with sniveling bed-wetters, but they are sniveling bed-wetters who have become accustomed to a lifestyle that rewards that behavior. They aren't willing to give up their lifestyle or professions without their version of a fight.

Donald Trump's political rise didn't change the MSM. Their version of the story is different, of course. They insist that what they've been up to since the 2016 campaign is merely a response to Trump's treatment of them.

The reality is that Trump exposed them for what they've been for over half of a century: partisan hacks who are more devoted to an agenda than seeking the truth like journalists of old.

For decades, Dan Rather was one of the most respected journalists and news anchors in America. In 2004, he was so eager to attempt to derail President George W. Bush's re-election that he ran with a story that was utter bullshit and was forced to resign in shame.

If the ones at the top are that tainted and agenda-driven, you can bet that the rank and file journos are all infected.

Rather, by the way, is still held in great esteem by almost all on the left.

Trump was the unfiltered kid who shouted to the crowd that America's Objective Media Emperor had no clothes.

What he had accomplished from the time that he announced his candidacy to the first months of his presidency was almost magical to a veteran media-basher like me.

People like me are limited to providing examples of media bias to make our point. The MSM in the United States has been doing the bias thing for so long that they are very adept at couching it. There are little things, like constantly labeling Republican politicians as "conservative" but never, ever mentioning that a liberal in Congress is, in fact, a liberal. Another trick is calling the conservative position on any issue "extreme." They have bags full of these tricks.

This subtlety on their parts makes it difficult at time to make the case about media bias. The tricks I cited above seem almost trivial. Their potency is derived from repetition.

Trump's victory was a one-two punch that laid bare the real agenda of the mainstream media in this country. Had he not won the election, the antics of theirs that he complained about during the campaign would have been dismissed in the media as the sour grapes of a candidate who knew that he was going to lose. It all would have been forgotten by now.

His triumph over Hillary Clinton not only gave him the grandest platform of all to keep pointing out the bias, but it created a complete meltdown on the part of the MSM that washed away all subtlety. Their toxic butthurt drove them to a point where all that mattered was destroying the man who made them feel that way. The bias was no longer veiled, and it was growing more obvious by the day.

The esteemed, low-functioning intellects of the Fourth Estate didn't see it that way at all. In the tiny minds of Club Journo, their daily Trump gripe collective was, and still is, the height of journalism.

In reality, it was more like the kids had been returned to their rightful place – a snot-nosed loser clique that sat on the fringe and made fun of the popular crowd who were living a better life. As long as they had each other they could reinforce the delusion.

Their behavior on social media was becoming a thing to behold. Rival news entities began pimping each other as far as anything having to do with Trump-bashing. The snot-nosed kids were doing an online version of laughing too loudly at things that weren't clever.

At some point in during the spring, I began describing this behavior by saying they were massaging each other with virtue lotion. They were so desperate to cling to their vestigial relevance in narrative dominance that they needed to constantly praise anyone in the clique for the Trump hate.

It went something like this. Someone from CNN would tweet something derogatory about the president. Generally, these tweets were opinionated observations and not anything having to do with actual reporting. Then someone from MSNBC would retweet it so quickly you'd think they were in bed with each other (not judging), often with a giddy comment added on in the hope of keeping the massage going. It usually would.

This cliquish behavior wasn't completely new with press. It was never as...eager before though.

It was pure delight observing how desperately they needed to constantly be validating one another. I keep all of the journos I watch in two different Tweetdeck columns and I was grateful that scratch 'n' sniff Internet isn't a thing yet because it would have all been reeking of flop sweat.

***

My fascination with the daily media virtue lotion massage was also serving to exorcise any emotions I had left for politics in general. I was paying attention to politics at least ten hours a day and not letting them affect me.

I was like a seven-year-old kid with an ant farm that I just couldn't stop staring at.

One of my favorite things to watch was their reactions to whether the president tweeted or not on any given Saturday morning.

The members of the media had long been expressing disdain for Trump's Twitter habit (which I will explore in a subsequent chapter). Because they are constitutionally incapable of self-awareness, they were doing it mostly on Twitter.

To them, it wasn't presidential for the most powerful man in the world to communicate however he damn well pleased. Never mind the fact that whenever President Obama would tweet anything they fell into an orgasmic frenzy that was so over the top it seemed as if the Emperor Caligula had come back to life and taken over the White House press pool.

Being Obama fans, what bothered them about Trump was his unfiltered honesty. When liberals and progressives are exposed to honesty, they react like a celiac sufferer who got drunk on beer and ate a loaf of bread. It's all diarrhea and depression after that.

President Trump had developed a habit of tossing out a couple of red meat-laden tweets early almost every Saturday morning. They were thought to be either amusing or incendiary depending on one's political persuasion. For the non-binary weirdos like me, they were usually both.

Within seconds, the wailing and gnashing of teeth over the un-presidential behavior would begin in the MSM.

That was to be expected.

More interesting were the Saturday mornings when the president didn't tweet anything. If it hit breakfast time on the east coast and the notorious early riser Trump hadn't offered a thought or two on Twitter the media would – in sync, of course

– begin noting the time and the lack of Twitter bombing from the White House.

There was a weird, scorned lover/stalker vibe to their behavior on these days. They *wanted* him to say something just so they could respond with a chorus of, "See how he is!" When he didn't, they seemed panicky, as if they were worrying that the ex-lover had completely moved on and was no longer giving any thought to them.

It had grown into a true "love to hate" relationship. The people in the mainstream media will never admit this, but President Trump, to paraphrase "Jerry Maguire," completes them.

This dynamic is even more obvious today but as I was watching it play out during the winter of 2017 it took me some time to realize that the absence of Trump's attention was a source of angst for the press puppies.

Once I finally put my finger on it, I began to ponder the reason or reasons for why it might be so.

It seemed unlikely that they would all be working through daddy issues, craving the attention of a patriarch who only spoke to them when had something critical to say because it was better than getting no attention at all.

As with anything having to do with political media in present day America, all roads lead back to Barack Obama.

The media's relationship with President Obama was so full of swooning giddiness that it was often uncomfortable to watch, even for those of us who were just there to mock them. One could almost picture them sobbing and hanging onto his ankles if he were to head for the door without saying good bye.

Obama was the left media's messiah, historic first, and prom king all at once. He could do almost no wrong. However, their loving gazes weren't returned by the man they spent their waking hours elevating to new heights.

He wasn't disdainful of the press, he just knew that they would be there for him no matter what. He knew he didn't have to be nice to them. He was the popular guy whose deepest relationships were with reflective surfaces and the media played the part of the homely girl who loved him and would jump to his side whenever he beckoned. When he didn't need her, he was barely aware of her existence.

Notoriously aloof,[15] their knee-weakening dreamboat never quite made them feel as loved as they felt they deserved to be.

Subconsciously smarting from this tragic eight year-long tale of unrequited love, the American political press in 2016 was the given a choice between another Democratic candidate who was even more distant, yet still expected things from them, and a guy who, for better or worse, wouldn't stop talking about them.

Long gone are the days when journalists referred to themselves as "this reporter" as they did everything possible to not be part of this story. The current crop all want to be an integral part of whatever it is they are pretending to report on. It's an exercise in painful-to-watch narcissism being done by people who for the most part don't possess enough talent to command attention.

They didn't want to spend any more time outside of the awareness of an aloof leader and found themselves – consciously or subconsciously – drawn to Trump.

---

[15] https://www.nytimes.com/2014/08/19/us/aloof-obama-is-frustrating-his-own-party.html

They loathed him but he was at least paying more attention to them than The Lightbringer ever did. It only took me a few Saturdays into the Trump presidency to see that the press was having abandonment flashbacks if the Big Guy didn't tweet.

It was absolutely precious.

The Saturday no-tweet angst was also a clear indication that the entire Trump tenure in office was going to be a "damned if he does, damned if he doesn't" affair as far as the press was concerned. Like the toddler who screams whether you're ignoring him or you attempt to console him, the emotionally challenged political media were never going to be satisfied by anything President Trump did.

The moment of that realization was when all of the magic began happening for me.

Sixteen
The Mother of All Sideshows

We have now arrived at the point in this journey where it all began to come together. I have, anyway.

This retrospective romp was designed to help me figure out just how my political pulse kept getting slower and calmer at a time in the country's history when being angry about everything became not just the norm, but practically required.

It was very necessary for me to go through the drama almost step-by-step to get a clear picture.

My very public departure from the Republican party was undoubtedly the official first step on my path to my state of political zero fucks to give. The feeling of freedom that gave me during the precise time in our quadrennial presidential election circus that typically brought me the most aggravation provided an unexpected beginning to a journey that I am still enjoying.

Had Granny Maojackets ascended to the office that she did so little to earn, I may have never completed more than the first part of the journey. I would have been in extreme opposition to the regime, more than likely unable to be free from frustration when reading or writing about its antics.

With Trump's victory I was given a great sense of relief that I wouldn't be living through another Clinton administration. That existential sigh afforded me the opportunity to take a "let's see what happens" approach to Trump's presidency.

That approach allowed me to drift over to a perspective that almost no one else in politics had, or even seemed to want.

While the majority of Americans who pay any attention to politics were laser-focused on every single move that President Trump made, I was looking in the other direction, riveted on the media's reaction to these moves. In practically no time at all, the particulars of what the president was doing or saying began to be irrelevant as far as I was concerned.

I cannot stress enough that this doesn't mean I was becoming apathetic for the first time in my life. Far from it. My, um, *wisdom*, was helping me with my new perspective. I've been around for more than a few presidents. The United States has survived a variety of potential and actual train wreck presidencies just since I've been here. As I am the product of an era when real American history was still taught in schools I have the added bonus of understanding that my beloved Republic has endured numerous shit shows that various presidents have dragged it into.

I didn't think that our new president was going to magically find a thread to pull that would finally unravel the fabric that the Constitution has kept woven together for so long.

The mainstream media clearly did believe that, however.

It was like putting thousands of people who suffer from severe aquaphobia on a yacht and sending it just far enough off shore that they could still actually wade in waist-deep water to the coastline but the only thing they would do was stare out to see and keep yelling that they were all going to die. No matter how big or small, every single wave brought new panic and terror.

In reality, ninety-nine percent of the waves weren't anything resembling big, but their irrational fear made it impossible to see that. The waves that were truly bigger than the rest still weren't very big.

None of that mattered. They all believed the same thing and they kept telling one another that the waves were gargantuan.

The yelling continued.

Trump had only been in office a few days when the press had already embarrassed themselves to the point where the Boy Who Cried Wolf could have wandered from fiction into reality and immediately have become the most credible journalist in America. Within a few months that yacht had been

137

floating in calm waters the entire time but the yelling hadn't dropped off so much as one decibel.

This is the part where I am admitting that I believe that many of them believed they had a reason to be afraid. They had been insulated in a like-minded cocoon for so long that they were now buying the bullshit stories they were paid to craft.

The once all-controlling media people were being freaked out by their own false narratives and yours truly suddenly couldn't think of anything else he wanted for his birthday or Christmas.

The president, his staff, and whatever they were or weren't doing every day were now just so much white (insert social justice warrior rant here) noise to me anymore.

My liberal friends would call or text me frequently, asking about whatever the president had most recently said or done and I would just shrug it off. Whatever it was, it wasn't going to be nearly as fun as watching Brian Stelter wet his Twitter pants for the third time that day just so Chuck Todd would reach across the professional aisle and give him virtual hand job to keep the boat full of aquaphobes screaming.

My ability focus on the mainstream media for the purpose of being able to continue commenting on and writing about them had the feel of being in the midst of a grand, long-running sociology experiment. Trump's daily/hourly input was merely part of the experiment. I truly was only interested in the reaction of the press.

After decades of being so biased and dishonest Donald Trump had singlehandedly turned the American political press into cartoonish parodies of themselves. The very people who had been able to spark anger in me with very little effort were now so over-the-top ridiculous that all I was interested in was seeing how far they would take it.

This is precisely what made me able to spend each day awash in political news and not let any of it affect me.

As one who'd been chronicling their awfulness for so long, I tended to rarely, if ever, believe the mainstream media whenever they were reporting on Republicans or conservatives. Their daily, anonymously sourced silver bullets that they all just knew were going to bring down the president weren't going to sway me.

Watching them fall all over themselves hoping that they would, however, was delightful.

As long as Trump didn't nuke my neighborhood I knew I was going to enjoy this show.

***

The media is so used to being surrounded by the safety of a non-thinking, uncritical echo chamber that they will occasionally be honest during one of their rare moments of lucidity. Every so often as the Trump Days wore on, someone in the MSM would admit in one way or another that they were being awful to him. It was rare, but it happened.

When it did, the briefly honest journo would offer the same weak rationalization: that they were only being awful because it was Trump, and he posed a unique threat to America.

This is an excuse that one might entertain for a minute or so but only if one had no experience with the mainstream media in the United States prior to 2009.

The mainstream media has been reflexively unfair to Republicans and conservatives since I have been involved in politics. The bias has only become more glaring and offensive in light of the treatment given the last two Democratic presidents.

The flipside to their treatment of Republicans is way they will champion virtually anything about their Democratic idols/deities. The slobbering crush the media had on President Obama has been well chronicled, but it was almost as bad when Bill Clinton was in office.

Clinton could do no wrong in the eyes of the media. Their current obsession with Trump's alleged extramarital affairs is ridiculous and meaningless for those of us who remember the Clinton administration. We were repeatedly (and I do mean repeatedly) told by members of both the political and entertainment media that a politician's private sexual escapades were none of the voters' business.

None.

The frequent addendum to that went something like this: "Only sexually repressed American conservative Christian prudes are still offended by things like this. We need to be more like Europe!"

While the ranks of all areas of media have been flooded with young talent they are still run by the people who spent years telling America that only Jesus freaks were concerned with Bill Clinton's sex life.

There has been a concerted effort on the part of the American left to undermine the family and marriage and now that Donald Trump is president they are really upset that their plan worked. Progressive history is one long lesson in "Be careful what you wish for," but, because they continually rewrite history, they never learn that.

The media's worshipful treatment of the only two Democrats in the last 38 years to occupy the White House is important to stress because it plays directly into how rotten they consistently treat Republican presidents.

The origins of it actually go back to John F. Kennedy. Thanks to the leftist inclinations of the media and academia, what the American public remembers about JFK's presidency is more of an American fairy tale than historical fact. The Kennedy era marked the first clear indications of the mainstream media's lurch to the left.

Having largely abandoned religion, liberals turn their politicians into idols to be worshipped. Since JFK's time, President Jimmy Carter is the only one who wasn't elevated to demigod status, probably because he's a devout Christian and the left isn't having any of that. It should be noted that in his later years Carter has greatly elevated his stature in the eyes of the MSM by become a consistent and prominent voice for people who hate Israel and love the Palestinians.

When a Republican ascends to the presidency Democrats and progressives no longer view their loss as simply the "win some, lose some" nature of our political system. They see it as an invasion of heretics who want to shred the canons of their secular church. Gone is any hope that they can adopt a "We'll get 'em next time!" attitude.

This perception of threat doesn't sit well with people who base their entire political belief system on emotion.

Thus, in their eyes every Republican president is not just a representative of the other dominant political party in the United States, but a demon interloper.

A DEMON, I SAY!

In their minds this not only gives them the right to speak of Republican presidents in the most insulting ways possible, but also gives them an obligation to do so. Liberals are forever dehumanizing their opponents so they can feel better about their own base, animalistic rage and responses.

They began practicing in earnest during the presidency of Ronald Reagan, whom they portrayed as a blithering idiot, wholly dependent on the thoughts of others around him. This became a core component of the media script for the future. Every Republican who manages to become the President of the United States is a barely-functioning moron who got lucky while the Democrats who make it are universally praised (within the ranks of the MSM, that is) as being towering intellects.

Left unchecked, they will still be writing the same script fifty years from now.

By the time the alleged idiot Reagan left office he had resurrected the economic shambles that Jimmy Carter had left behind, done the heavy lifting that would lead to the end of the Cold War, and laid the groundwork for the science fiction-like missile defense system that protects us today.

This country would be even more blessed than it already is if every president were that stupid.

Rhodes Scholar genius Bill Clinton thought the President of the United States could have an affair with a young intern and she would keep her mouth shut about it and not tell her friends.

George W. Bush was savaged far more by rank and file Democrats and the media. Not only was he another demon Republican interloper, but Democrats truly believed that he had stolen the election. He didn't but, being the huge fans of revisionist historical fiction that they are, Democrats to this day believe he did.

Perhaps the nicest thing that Democrats ever said about Bush when he was in office was that he was dumb. Never mind that he had an undergrad degree from Yale and an MBA from Harvard, he's a Republican so academic achievements don't count. In the Democratic version of such tales, Republicans who graduate from Ivy League schools only do so because they are pedigreed legacies, while Democrats from one of the Ivies got through because they are the greatest geniuses of their day.

I say that is the nicest thing they said, because when they weren't calling Bush stupid, they were calling him Hitler. The "we're only being this awful because it's Trump" argument is somewhat weakened by this fact.

In all fairness, members of the media weren't calling Bush Hitler, but they weren't *not* calling him Hitler either. Whenever anyone so much as hiccupped in the direction of President Obama, the media would immediately brand him or her as proof positive that the Klan was riding again in America.

When George W. Bush effigies were being burned all the while he was being compared to a genocidal maniac, the press was suddenly unable to put on its journalism pants and write any stories about it.

A Republican doesn't really have to win the presidency to receive the unbalanced wrath of the MSM. Trump-era revisionist history finds Democrats praising Mitt Romney as the kind of decent man that Trump could never dream of being.

When Romney was the 2012 GOP nominee, however, the press devoted months trying to convince the public that Mitt was a high school bully, an animal abuser and, when those didn't seem awful enough, that he was responsible for giving a woman cancer.

That's how they treat the "nice guys."

First and foremost, the mainstream media hates Donald Trump because he's a Republican president. They can shriek "But this time it's different," all they want to, but the only real change is that the level of shrillness has gone up several notches. Trump makes them lose the thin veneer of professionalism that they have been trained to use to hide their bias.

It isn't simply Trump's ability to unmask the perpetually disingenuous American political press that appeals to those of us who have been worn out by decades of bias, it's also the fact that he is utterly remorseless and gleeful while doing so.

Congressional Republicans and Republican presidents throughout the years have acknowledged that the press has two different approaches to dealing with the major parties and that they aren't on the good end of the deal.

Almost to a man and woman they've been unwilling to fight back.

From time to time, a Republican politician will call out the MSM. The skirmish is always brief, generally ending with the pol just letting it go and the media emboldened after having scared another one away.

Over the years I have gotten excited when one of these Republicans would tease and seem as if he or she were ready to hold the media accountable. I am always disappointed. They may still mildly protest the inherent bias, but it doesn't happen often, and there are never specifics involved.

Trump not only continually points out the media's ever-growing pile of biased lies, he is willing to call them lies.

Halle-freakin'-lujah.

After decades of watching 99.9% of the Republican politicians in Washington either tacitly or joyfully (see: "Jeff Flake") acting like fawning little bitches for the mainstream media Trump's justified contempt for them is a daily blast of cold-beer-on-a-hot-day refreshment I have yet to tire of.

***

The press has taken to describing President Trump's willingness to fight back as a "threat to journalism and freedom of the press."

The only real threat to journalism in America are the people who continue to pass along agenda-driven speculation as "news."

That is all.

***

Even though this battle is obviously the focal point of my enjoyment of this hot mess I call it a sideshow because that is all it is to me. The entertainment value it provides me is wonderful, but peripheral. I can watch when I want and easily return to whatever the main attraction of the day is. That varies, but I promise that it is never political.

Trump vs the media is a spectacle I can't help but watch without a slight smile, and I hate to smile. There may even be an almost permanent twinkle in my eyes at this point. I'm unfamiliar with this feeling, of course. Politics has provided all kinds of things for me in my life, but never calm and joy. I usually have to day drink to get that.

Now I can watch the daily press meltdowns on Twitter while day drinking.

God bless America.

Also...be right back.

Seventeen

ZOMG CONSTITUTIONAL CRISIS

The American Democrat/Progressive/Tree-humping left has become fond of saying that things they don't like about Trump all portend a constitutional crisis.

They don't.

Glad we cleared that up.

Eighteen

Always Say Never Again

Like the leftist media, my friends in the Never Trump crowd were busy exhibiting their displeasure at the state of Oval Office occupancy in 2017. There were differences in how they went about it that, as time wore on, became less and less discernible.

The Nevers weren't looking for a magic election do-over pill like the lefties were. They just wanted to make sure that everybody was clear on the fact that they didn't support Trump before or after the election. To this end they accomplished something previously thought impossible: they became even whinier than the left.

Perhaps I should say that many of them did. There were, and still are, a few different membership tiers in the Never Trump treehouse. They are as follows.

Tier 3-Safe Cover

These are people who usually would vote but didn't in 2016 because they didn't like Trump and couldn't remember if the Super Magical Spy who was supposed to save them was Gary Johnson or Evan McMullin. They remain in the Never crowd just so their liberal mommy blogger friends will still drink sangria with them.

Tier 2-Principled Pugnacity

The PPs are the Republicans who spent most of 2016 assuring everyone there was no way that Trump would be elected. Post-election they remain opposed to everything that the president does because, as they will repeatedly tell any stranger within earshot, their principles are super strong and unyielding. These principled paragons of conservatism remain in the Never crowd just so their new liberal blogger BFFs will drink sangria with them.

Tier 1-CNN Boner

This highest level of treehouse access is for people who are an even louder version of the Tier 2 members but also experience an almost sexual response to any negative news about Trump that's reported by news organizations that they abhorred just three years ago. Tier 1 members remain in the Never Crowd just so Ana Navarro will one day drink sangria with them.

A shadow group of Never Trump people also exist. It consists mostly of anti-Trump Republicans and conservatives who work in some form of media and remain opposed to Trump but don't brandish the #NeverTrump hashtag as if it were given to them by the archangel Michael. They don't have a name and aren't granted access to the treehouse for the weekly "Wolf Blitzer's Dreamiest Moment" vote.

Not to be outdone by-and as a sign of their increasing similarity to-the left media, the more prominent voices among the Never Trump crowd developed a virtue lotion of their own. Like their buddies on the left, they spent countless hours a day slathering it upon one another on social media, just with less implied giggling. These are, after all, people who want to be seen as a wise elder council. They are more into implied smirking with an occasional "Pshaw!" added for emphasis.

The level of commitment of the Never crowd should not be underestimated. Friendships have been fractured and professional relationships strained or dissolved in the name of Never purity.

I've spent decades as an arch-conservative in the entertainment industry. For the uninitiated, there aren't many of us in that line of work. Still, I have managed to get along with my ideological opposites without losing friends.

That hasn't been the case with the Nevers. People whose company I used to greatly enjoy-some of whom I considered good friends-aren't happy with the fact that I won't engage in 24/7 Trump hate. They no longer speak to me. One even told me to go fuck myself after I gave him some gentle ribbing on Twitter about the frequency of his anti-Trump tweets. It was the only political disagreement we'd experienced in nine years of knowing each other.

But principles or something.

***

I wasn't always this derisive of the Never Trump people and I should make it clear that I don't feel this way about all of them. I work and am still friends with a lot of Republicans and conservatives who can't stand Trump. The difference between them and the ones who no longer speak to me is that they have professional and personal interests beyond hating Trump.

The hashtag Never Trump people, however, have deeply invested almost everything about themselves into hating every single thing the president-or anybody connected to him-does. It's a reverse cult of personality, featuring an object of derision as its focus rather than an object of affection.

On their best days, the cult is tedious; on their worst, pathological. It's very uncomfortable watching people I once hung out with and respected acting like they have been body snatched by a bunch of bitchy little Salon.com interns.

We get it, you don't like Trump.

That doesn't mean you're a better person than the people who voted for him, it just means you backed a loser in the last election. That happens to almost half of the electorate every election. The adults move on.

They don't spend every day after the election screeching about their dissatisfaction all the while convincing themselves that the reason they're doing it is because they are, in fact, the adults.

It's difficult to lecture others about your couth, comportment, and superior principles while in the midst of a tantrum that has been going on for a year and a half (as of the time of this writing).

To the hardcore hashtag crowd, I'm an unprincipled sellout because I'll give Trump a nod when he does something like appoint a constitutional conservative to an appellate court. As far as the Never Trump purists are concerned, something like that counts for nothing because "DAMN IT HE EMBARRASSED US WHEN HE WON!"

A rational, truly principled conservative would think that having a slew of conservative judges who will be in the judiciary long after Trump is out of office is far better than whatever activist havoc Hillary Clinton would be wreaking in the courts were she in the Oval Office.

The fact that I won't have to worry about a bunch of Clinton-appointed judicial crusaders legalizing abortion until the mother's water breaks and labeling every pro-Second Amendment word out of my mouth as "hate speech" covers a multitude of Trump sins in my book. With these worries removed, I wouldn't care if Trump spent every day eating Big Macs in his underwear on live television while tweeting a barrage of insults about Jim Acosta being in various compromising positions with farm animals.

At this point in my life, after having endured hundreds (thousands, maybe) of ineffective Republican nice guys in Washington who never did anything for me or the country I want Donald Trump on that wall.

At least when it comes to appointing judges.

A Never purist can't even give grudging praise to President Trump for the work he's doing appointing judges. Sure, he'll be thrilled in eight years when he's not being put in jail for thought crimes because Trump saved the judiciary from progressivism, but today he can only focus on the raging case of ass-chafe he's had since November 8th, 2016.

The Never Trump types who will give the president credit for such things usually only do so after hedging the grudging credit with so many disclaimers that you wish Trump Steaks were still a thing so you could shove some in their mouths just to make them stop.

It bears repeating that I didn't vote for Trump largely because I thought he would never do anything that could remotely be construed as conservative. I thought he was a Democratic wolf in Republican sheep's clothing.

Every time he does something like get a Don Willett on a circuit court it's like a mini-political Christmas for me. I can't imagine being so invested in indignation that I wouldn't enjoy the good stuff.

And I'm kind of a dick.

***

I would also like to point out that I am aware that there is also a very large cult of personality that is pro-Trump. The original MAGA people are all in. I have said since the early Obama days that I'm uneasy with the cult of personality stuff no matter who it grows around. Politicians are not heroes to be worshipped. They're our employees.

That's a different book though.

***

This is supposed to be a journey to figure out how I hit and maintained my new political sense of chill. Thus far this chapter just seems like I want to beat up on some of the Never

Trump crowd, but I actually do have a reason for going into detail about them.

As the Never Trump reaction stayed strong and, in too many cases, got personal, I was getting a glimpse of an emotional place where I never,ever want to be.

True, my lefty friends in entertainment are in a state of perma-anger about Trump's election, but I long ago got used to them being angry about anything any Republican did. It's what I expect from them. As I never plan on accomplishing anything with them politically, I mostly just tune them out.

The Never Trump anger made me reassess why I would want to be involved in politics as an activist ever again.

American conservatives are a loose collection of people occupying various places that are decidedly to the right of America's political center. We just sort of hang on to each other every few years to try and win an election or two. One of the very few things that united hardcore conservatives in recent years was disdain for moderate Republicans (generally consultants and Beltway types) and an overwhelming contempt for the mainstream media.

At CPAC 2017 I found myself listening to a conservative Never Trump friend praising the real journalism that CNN and company were doing now that Trump was in office.

This was a guy I had known for almost eight years and had always counted among those I'd want on my short list of people for the activist trenches.

He was now a CNN fan boy.

I had a brief discussion with him, pointing out that he was rather new to the idea than any journalism at all was being done on CNN or MSNBC. He tried to defend his position, saying that we should celebrate the fact that we they were finally getting around to it. I was about to explain why he was full of shit but realized that there was free booze, walked away, and never looked back.

As the Trump era moved through its first full year, more of my conservative Never friends got really comfortable with establishment moderate Republicans they wouldn't have offered a half of a nacho to three years earlier.

Seriously, why waste nachos on a squish?

The lines had been redrawn. No longer were we divided into conservatives and moderates, it was now Never Trump and pro-Trump.

The worst part was that those in the conservative Never crowd were conferring principled conservative status on moderates who had done nothing for years but fail ideological purity litmus tests given by the very people who were now welcoming them.

Mildly put, I didn't have time for that crap.

I also didn't let it bother me for long. The realization that one of the few political constants I could take comfort in was now gone was the last little piece to my freedom puzzle.

My untethering from the Republican party had given me the freedom to float around in a state of discovery, and that had made for a pleasant journey. Seeing so many legitimate conservatives don their fire-retardant strange bedfellows pajamas and hop in the sack with the squishy mods was the last little thing I needed to free me from the pangs of activism.

If people I had trusted to have my political back for so long were now singing the praises of CNN and frolicking ever so gleefully with the bland, ineffective wing of the GOP I knew I'd never jump into a serious activist battle again.

This was a key component to breaking my emotional attachment to politics even while I was reading and writing about them almost every day.

I'm not happy that I had to lose friends for this to happen but lemons and lemonade or something.

Thanks, #NeverTrump-you finally accomplished something!

***

It's difficult to see where all of this Never rift stuff goes in the future. It's not unnatural for conservatives to fight among ourselves. We get past it and form yet another uneasy political alliance because we're more worried about the leftist nightmare looming on the other side.

Unfortunately, a lot of the Nevers are gleefully cavorting with some of the Nightmares. I'm not clear on how the supposed rock-ribbed conservative principles fit into that equation. If you're the go-to "conservative" Trump-hater for any mainstream outlet you need to get to Bed, Bath & Beyond to see if they sell any ideological mirrors you can hang up and gaze into. Perhaps you'll get your bearings again.

Unless the Democrats and their press monkeys succeed in dismantling this presidency, Trump will likely be the nominee in 2020. I say "likely" because I honestly thought he would get bored with this gig pretty quickly.

I think he's starting to like it though.

Should he again be on the ballot then this divide between the pro-Trump people of varying levels of enthusiasm and the Never Trump people is bound to worsen.

When conservatives and Republicans have fought in the past, it's generally only for one election cycle. Now we are potentially looking at eight years of some pretty nasty invective being hurled back and forth (yes, both sides do it).

I don't know if we will all be able to put aside the acrimony and unite behind the historic Nikki Haley-Ivanka Trump ticket in 2024.

Nineteen
TWITTERPOCALYPSE

There was one thing I admired Trump for from the earliest days of the 2016 campaign: his use of social media.

Until April of 2016, I was doing regular (twice-weekly) political commentary on an online video channel called PJTV. I frequently commended Trump's ability to connect with voters using the most popular media of the day. By the beginning of 2016 I was insisting that Trump's employment of Twitter and Facebook as one of the ways to distinguish himself from the crowded Republican primary field would one day soon be taught in Political Science programs at universities all over the country.

That's what I felt even when I didn't think he was going to win.

His victory, and subsequent use of Twitter to circumvent a hostile press and communicate directly with the American people should make it required learning in every Poli-Sci program in the United States.

Unlike a lot of people in my age range-ish I have long been a fan of the non-Facebook social media options. MySpace had page templates for comedians, so a lot of us experimented with it early on. I started using it in earnest in early 2005, I think. As a joke, I recently checked my account. It's still there and it still has around 17,000 "friends" on it. Sadly, my brilliant, and somewhat psychotic "About Me" section was lost to the new format.

Twitter tells me that I joined in January of 2008 but I don't remember using it much until right around election time that year.

I was doing a lot of political blogging then on my own site. For free.

Yeah, I hated 2008.

Someone who was a lot more involved in blogging than I was then suggested I use Twitter to promote my posts and I took his advice. I have no idea how many followers I had in the fall of 2008 but I'm sure it was in the low hundreds, if that many. As promotional tools went, the price was right so I didn't worry too much about reach.

After the election I had far too much time on my hands because the economic crisis hit stand-up pretty hard too. I was obviously upset by Obama's victory and my only real outlet (as a rational grown up) was to vent online. I blogged more, posted on Twitter more and when I wasn't either of those things I just began adding as many Twitter followers as I could.

I would love to say that I was doing that because I'm some sort of digital media wiz and saw where Twitter was heading but mostly it was because I didn't have much work and was bored.

Twitter exploded as a community building and news gathering tool for those of us involved in the Tea Party movement. I co-founded the first Los Angeles Tea Party with three other people and I'd never met any of them in person until the day of the event. It was all done via Twitter.

I mention all of this just to establish that I have been aware of the platform's political uses and power almost from my earliest days of using it. Candidate Trump's deployment of it as a political weapon in the campaign didn't seem odd to me. It was the natural evolution of political messaging as far as I was concerned.

In my professional and personal circles I was a voice praising Trump alone in the wilderness then.

I am not even sure Trump's most avid supporters grasped the genius of his social media strategy at first. They were paying attention to his tweeting though.

To most of the rest of the American electorate, Trump's no-filter tweeting was yet another habit that made him too crass to be president.

The octogenarians-before-their-time Smoking Jacket wing of the Republican party really didn't like Trump's Twitter habit. These are a bunch of 30 and 40-somethings who act as if they were brought up through the ranks in Ike's GOP. They are basically living specimens of the left's caricature of conservatives. Thankfully, there aren't too many of them but when they have one of their stuffy snits it does choke off a lot of oxygen in the room.

If 21st Century Americans weren't such spoiled, chronic complainers, Trump's almost complete bypassing of traditional media political advertising would have been embraced by people who weren't even supporting him.

The scourge of any political campaign is the advertising onslaught that voters are subjected to. Radio ads, television ads, robocalls, billboards...everyone hates them. Let's be honest with ourselves: elections are like having a meal that you hate the taste of but know is good for you forced upon you. The advertising and robocalls make them feel like the meal is being served by a sweaty waiter who has severe body odor that the other patrons can smell, halitosis, and, worst of all, keeps hanging around your table to talk to you.

In 2016 Trump fired the waiter.

In a restaurant full of sane people, this would have been applauded by almost everyone dining there. Instead, they just complained about how rude the manager was.

Trump was spending so little on conventional campaign advertising at one point that the know-it-all Never Trump Republican consultant types were assuring us that fact alone had already doomed any chance he had of winning.

The disdain that consultants had for Trump's direct approach was understandable, however. They were the middle men being cut out. Staring at a not-too-distant future where candidates no longer fork over massive retainers to consultants who bleed the campaign dry by spending what money is left on crappy ads and mailers was disconcerting to them. Trump's use of a 21st Century medium to get his message out was a direct threat to a political business model that hadn't changed much at all since the 1970's.

If it hasn't been made clear by now, I should just go ahead and say it: I don't like political consultants very much. If a new trend in politics upsets them, I'm generally in favor of it. Perhaps the reason that I was an early fan of Trump's Twitter escapades is because they were annoying the GOP squish consultant class.

***

Obviously, Donald Trump wasn't the first political candidate on Twitter. Social media has been a part of campaigning for several years.

The standard model of social media usage for politicians is that a perky millennial who "gets Twitter" runs the account for Senator Luddite, posting bland statements that all read as if they'd been pulled from a direct mail campaign targeting nonagenarians. It's not unlike making a television commercial that does nothing put point a camera at a billboard for sixty seconds. The senator will then tweet something on his own, usually something benign like congratulating an athlete and done under the strict supervision of the perky millennial. He usually adds his initials so that everyone can see that he left the Senate Dining Room and got in front of a computer like a regular man of the people.

Even Barack Obama-the super hippest godlike POTUS in the history of the universe-didn't do all of his own tweeting.

What set Trump apart as a candidate and now as a politician is that he gets Twitter as well as the perky millennials do.

Twitter isn't like other social media, and I'm mostly talking about Facebook here.

It moves faster, which is why it's a great news source. It is leaner than other social media, even with the expanded character count. It's made for stream-of-consciousness material, not scripted messaging.

Donald Trump was made for Twitter and Twitter was made for Donald Trump.

The very thing that most people complain about Trump doing on Twitter is what makes him so good on the platform.

Detractors and even people on his side often say they wish he wouldn't tweet whatever pops into his head. That, however, is exactly what Twitter is best for.

As of the time I am writing this, I have tweeted over 193,000 times. That's really not much-I have friends who are well beyond the 300K and 400K marks. You don't crank out content like that by putting a lot of thought into each tweet. In fact, if I begin to type a tweet and think it over long enough to maybe want to edit it I usually just scrap the whole thing.

Imagine being in a conversation with someone who pauses and thinks for thirty seconds before every response he makes. You will either fall asleep or be arrested for strangling the guy. That's what the canned, scripted overthinkers on Twitter are like. They are somewhere else though so you can't strangle them, which makes them all the more annoying.

President Trump understands what the Twitter standard operating procedure is. If you wake up and think of something to tweet don't think about whether you should tweet it, just tweet it. If you happen to be the President of the United States then *really fucking tweet it*.

What Trump the candidate did was impressive enough, but his presidential tweets have been even more trailblazing in the world of political communication.

As always, Trump's real value for me is directly linked to how much aggravation he causes the media. His Twitter habit as president has probably tripled the number of Xanax prescriptions written for people who work in the Washington bureaus of the major news agencies.

After decades of seeing the press spin positively or negatively-but rarely believably-for presidents depending on their party, watching Trump bypass the media as if they weren't even there has been one of the most refreshing things I've ever seen. That he does it on a platform run by a leftist billionaire who wants to shut up anyone who disagrees with him makes me wish he would tweet a lot more.

Trump has reimagined FDR's fireside chats for the 21st Century. The chats are super short and lacking ambiguity for the most part. The president tweets, the people read, and everyone is pretty clear on what just happened. No need to convene a panel of pundits to tell the American people what he meant. It's just one more thorn in the seemingly endless supply he has to stick in the sides of the MSM.

In the television era the president's opportunities (when not campaigning) to speak to the American people are usually as follows: times of crisis, one-on-one interviews given to TV journalists, the State of the Union address, or press conferences. Rallies are sprinkled in there (Trump is and Obama was very fond of them), but they aren't often broadcast to a wide audience or in their entireties.

The State of the Union is a bloated beast that's boring to listen to even for the supporters of the president in office at the time. By the time the seventeen thousandth contrived applause break hits, most Americans are wondering if anyone at urgent care can legally put them into a medical coma until the clapping stops.

Times of crisis are no fun because often everyone is rallying around the president and unity is a real snoozer. Glad my parents never tried it.

The interviews are where the media really gets to shine. When talking to a Democratic president they can make him seem flawless by lobbing softballs the whole time.

"What is your greatest achievement so far as president and why will it only get better?"

"Nice tie. Can I touch it?"

There is a decided shift in tone when interviewing a Republican POTUS, however.

"Racist or rapist?"

While the president in question is obviously able to answer in his own words, the overall perception can be greatly shaped by the questions.

A favorite tactic is insisting that a Republican (president or candidate) disavow someone that he has nothing to do with but with whom the press wants to create the illusion of a connection simply be asking the question.

The goal is always to trip up a Republican so the media can get a "Gotcha!" moment to repeat on a loop for a news cycle or two, while making the Democrat feel like he's getting a massage. If you think I am making this up, remember that a New York Times reporter once asked President Obama what "enchanted" him the most about being president. It was like watching a teenage fan zine interview a pop star. He was a journalist representing the most influential news organization in America while talking to the country's first African-American president after his first 100 days in office and *that* is what he came up with.

The game is always rigged against a Republican when a member of the mainstream media is asking the questions, so interviews are the some of the worst ways for the public to see them.

Trump took the fat out of this process like a cosmetic surgeon using a hose the size of the Lincoln Tunnel for liposuction.

Watching President Trump tweet about the news that he knows his supporters care about-rather than what the MSM wants people to care about-is the closest that modern

Americans will get to having frequent chats with the chief executive. Back before we got so assassination happy, the citizens of this great land could walk into the White House and chat with their leader. I don't know if that really helped the country to function better-we did end up having a civil war after all-but it's nice to feel wanted.

With Twitter Trump is creating the illusion and feeling that he is Joe Voter's buddy at the bar, just kicking back and having a beer with him. He pulls this off even though he doesn't drink and in his real social circles no "Joseph" is ever called "Joe." It doesn't matter though, he obviously wants to connect with the American people without a lot of interference. It's not his fault that the whinier among us don't want him to.

It is stunning to me that people outside of the media wouldn't want the president to communicate in a direct fashion using something like Twitter. Are we really so hung up on the notion of "presidential" behavior that we prefer there be a lot of buffers between us and the person in charge? I'm not European, I don't need a figurehead steeped in tradition and bullshit decorum.

I want to know what's on my president's mind.

Not only do I not think Trump's Twitter routine is something that's unbecoming for a president, I think every president going forward should be required to tweet even more than he does. At least until Twitter is replaced by some kind of brain implant telepathy thing, that is. I don't want information filtered through White House correspondents, I want POTUS live-tweeting state dinners and policy meetings.

I cannot overemphasize how clueless I think people who say Trump should lay off Twitter are. It doesn't matter whether they are Republicans or Democrats.

CLUELESS.

After the ugliness of the primaries, Republican National Convention, and the general election there was obviously a lot of friction between the new president and many members of his own party. There were a lot of nervous grins in the early days of the Trump administration whenever Republican members of Congress were asked about him. One popular refrain then was, "Well, I wish he wouldn't tweet so much."

Idiots.

After being blind-sided by Trump's lack of conventionality they were still doddering around and saying, "Gosh darn it, I wish he would quit with the newfangled stuff!"

I had never been more comfortable with my decision to leave the party.

On more than one occasion I wrote that if the GOP knew what was good for it they would not only stop whining about Trump and Twitter but they would ask him to teach them how to use it properly.

Somewhere in the distance a Republican consultant with a 1-3 record in elections is screaming, "BUT DIRECT MAIIIIIIILLLLLLL!"

The GOP will probably never learn any lessons from Trump's victory because they ended up being the winning party despite themselves. They will get dragged along for the ride again in 2020. Expect the Republican brain trust to continue partying like it's 1969 after Trump is gone though.

If, however, they do take some Twitter lessons from him I may consider voting for more of them in the future.

If they don't, I will probably write in "Ghost of Thomas Jefferson" for my remaining presidential elections.

***

One last important by-product of President Trump's Twitter usage needs to be mentioned. It is never discussed by his Republican and conservative haters, probably because they remain so worked up that they don't take time to ponder such things.

Social media-and Twitter in particular-have a history of targeting conservatives for suspension and, often, complete banning.

Twitter co-founder and CEO Jack Dorsey is an avowed leftist and he does nothing to hide his contempt for anything he deems wrong thought. He is also a coward.

Dorsey is quick to publicly crow about any measures Twitter is taking to police and correct the behavior of its users. Those measures usually sound like they were fed to him by an angry college-aged Feminist Studies Social Justice Warrior, who in turn is the puppet of a professor who spends her free time making penises out of papier-mâché which she burns in effigy every night.

I am not saying that Jack Dorsey is a pissed off lesbian but I'm not saying he isn't one either.

In almost ten years of heavy Twitter usage I have yet to see any of the rules regarding abuse apply to people on the left. Vile threats leveled at conservative women go unpunished while people on my side of the aisle are suspended or banned for saying something that is usually true but not politically correct.

I had planned on writing this section anyway but, as fate would have it, I woke up this morning to find my Twitter account "restricted" for the first time ever. I hadn't heard of anyone being restricted before today. I have access to my account but I can't tweet or retweet anything. If I try, I get an error message that the tweet has been "flagged as suspicious."

My Twitter habits haven't changed, kids. I did, however, write a blog post yesterday in response to Dorsey's announcement of new rules, which he ominously said would focus on behavior rather than content. I also mentioned Dorsey's continually uneven application of the rules already in place.

Twitter never responds to inquiries from any of the people I know who have been suspended so I am left to infer away as to what is happening.

I could say that my "restricted" status coming less than a day after I wrote that post is coincidence but I don't believe in coincidence.

Angry Jack is up to his purging tricks again.

This problem may become even worse for conservatives under the recently announced rules, which is why I wrote the post in the first place.

The thing I mentioned early that no one talks about is the fact that there is one center-right person the cowardly Dorsey won't dare ban from Twitter: the Republican President of the United States.

Twenty
Day Drinking

Throughout the time it has taken me to write this I have been worried that the political perpetually pissed off attitude that is gripping the nation would finally saunter over to my table and make itself known in a way I couldn't unknow. This feeling kept plaguing me even though it has been almost two years since my emotions checked the hell out of Hotel Aggravation. A lot of personal crap has happened in the interim which probably should have permanently soured my mood. (I won't go into that here, you'll have to see me live to find out how those demons get exorcised.) Yet here I still am, detached and loving it.

When I decided to write this, I wasn't really looking for an epiphany that I might have missed. I don't believe people have epiphanies anymore. Maybe some who have been through a tragedy still do but the rest of us are rather epiphany free. St. Paul probably had the last really good one and that was so long ago even Dianne Feinstein wasn't alive. I honestly wasn't aware of all of the particulars that me transform from a guy who always wanted to throw his computer through a window to one who is in a permanent "third beer while day drinking" state of chill.

You day drinkers know what I mean.

The first beer of any day drinking session serves one of two purposes: refreshment or stress relief. It is usually consumed rather quickly. One generally doesn't plan on spending the day drinking at this point. One beer can't hurt though, right?

The second beer is ordered without a thought as to whether it should be or not. Beer One hasn't had the time to kick in and take care of what it was intended for so the Beer Two is needed as a kind of booster to help Beer One realize its full potential.

Beer Three is where all of the real day drinking magic happens and is the closest thing to irrefutable proof of the existence of God that I've personally encountered.

The Beer Two booster has done its job and is now washing the waves of a glorious sunlit buzz over your previously un-buzzed life. You wonder if it can get any better. From just beyond the tap, Beer Three says, "Yes, yes it can."

It's at that moment when you go from wondering if you should have another one to trying to remember if you ever lived on a planet or in a time where and when you shouldn't.

The Third Beer Buzz makes you feel that every decision you've made that day is has been the perfect one. You become relaxed, detached, and begin having a ball watching everyone around you, no matter what kind of mood they seem to be in.

Everything about the Trump Era so far has been one long political day-drinking Third Beer Buzz for me.

I'm in the middle of the chaos six days a week (I avoid politics on Sundays) but none of it gets to me. The daily outrage washes over me and doesn't bother me at all because I have reached an almost unnerving state of calm on the inside. There are days that I am so detached and free from emotion that I wonder if someone can become a sociopath, and wonder if I am that someone.

Many people tell me that they are going through the same thing, but they really aren't. They've usually checked out of politics completely. I'm still reading political news and writing about it for several hours a day, sometimes as many as twelve. Three of the five Twitter columns I monitor all day on Tweetdeck are political news feeds broken up in different ways.

I consume as much political news and information now as I did five years ago when I was still a passionate activist, but once I am done for the day it gets shut down harder than a frat boy hitting on a super model.

I have an "Off" switch now.

I didn't used to have one because I was a dedicated activist. There was always another fight. I talked about politics at parties. There was a lot of plotting and planning, as well as a focused fervor to keep honed. It's a tough gig being a conservative in California. One has to stay sharp and alert for that.

Most of the discoveries I have made for myself in writing this are about getting away from political activism in one way or another.

My split with the Republican party was obviously the first big step. Even though that was a move that came about as a result of despair and disillusionment, the freedom that followed made it a positive experience.

Once I no longer had any emotional investment in the party, I didn't have to worry about being disappointed by it again. After thirty years of being Charlie Brown to the GOP's Lucy, I told her to take her football and shove it up her ass.

Damn, that felt good.

President Trump has done more to expose the borderline un-American bias in the mainstream media than all of us who have been writing about it for years could. It was media bias that first compelled me to write about politics. Trump's got that now. I can order another beer.

It is the Never Trump conservatives who made my break from activism final and irrevocable.

Seeing so many people with whom I had shared a common cause for so long quickly align themselves with those we all considered the opposition killed off whatever bits of political idealism that may have been floating around inside of me. That they were do it in the name of conservative principles brought it to a level of ridiculousness that I was left with no choice but to laugh at myself for having ever taken them seriously.

Once more: the hardcore Never Trump "conservatives" are not operating from a place of conservative principle. If you find yourself in sync with the CNN types several times a day you may very well still be principled, but in no context can your principles be construed as "conservative." Conservatives don't suck up to people who would prefer that conservatives never be heard from again.

When #NeverTrump was born, a thousand new David Gergens were minted overnight. Neither the media nor conservatism need that.

After seeing people I once thought I shared an ideological bond with head for a part of the political spectrum we used to take pride in fighting it's safe to say that I developed some trust issues.

I won't be doing any group things (sounds dirty but isn't) again.

Knowing that I will no longer be dealing with the kind of aggravation that comes from hoping to affect change in Washington, D.C. makes the days really, really pleasant.

Earlier this year whenever anyone asked me if I was going to CPAC I kept replying, "Why would I?" I had already moved well beyond any desire to be part of a bigger political movement and I thought it was weird that others still wanted to.

After one friend asked, I said "Unless there's an extraordinary amount of money involved, I can't imagine ever going to another political conference again." He was stunned and thought I might be kidding. He then hit me with the excuse everyone uses for CPAC: that it's nice just to see everyone and hangout.

Half the people I used to like to see and hangout with now look at Jake Tapper like he's internet porn and they're 13-year-old boys.

I'll pass.

The thing that was a big part of my adult life is gone and I'm not upset about it. It was fun at times but ultimately frustrating. If I had known getting away from it would be this relaxing I probably would have bugged out in 2012. That's when I first seriously considered it but, for reasons that still aren't clear to me, I decided to stick around for more Republican futility.

Now that I am free from activism I am no longer burdened by idealistic expectations. When the expectations go, so do stress, disappointment, and the desire to live in an abandoned mine shaft just to avoid people.

(Note: I still avoid people, I'm just slightly less Unabomber creepy about it.)

***

It would be very remiss of me to not spend some time dwelling on the great part my friends on the Democrat/progressive side of the aisle have played in bringing me to this place of happy clouds and endless daytime Third Beers.

I have been a professional entertainer since I was in my twenties, so I have spent most of my adult life in an industry where I am surrounded by liberals. We have all managed to play nice and that's not because I am a shrinking violet who kept his mouth shut. My politics have always been known to my comedian friends and acquaintances.

Most of us are products of a bygone era in American politics though.

Back in Ancient Times, Democrats and Republicans were allowed to vehemently disagree about politics but still be friends.

Weird, I know, but I swear to all of my younger readers that I am not making this up.

I know that I just said that I get along with my liberal comedian friends, but that's a very select group. We tend to bond as comics first, and that gives us a lot to unite around because were a weird little offshoot of polite society. They politics are almost secondary for comedians of a certain age, even if we're passionately political. We can argue about taxes for a while, then get back to road stories about club owners we hate. Shared occupational hatred is a great bonding mechanism.

On a larger scale, progressive Americans are trying to teach young children (via public education) that people who vote like I do are child-murdering Nazis who rape the planet in our spare time. That would be one of the more favorable descriptions, by the way.

I was a Psychology major but I dropped out of college to do stand-up. Had I stayed in school and gotten a PhD I wouldn't be able to help these people with their lunacy. Nor would I want to.

If you sat a ten-year-old kid in front of me and asked me to explain what I don't like about liberalism, I could coherently explain it all, citing historical example after historical example, and finish it all with a supply of anecdotal evidence based on thirty years of experience just as a flourish.

Send that same kid over to a present day American liberal and have him expound on what he dislikes about conservatives and he'll explain my well-founded distrust of government and taxation by telling the child that I hate poor people.

Clarifying: the only time I have ever hated poor people is when I was poor and engaging in the self-loathing that is common among comedians. I have no beef with the rest of them.

I have no desire to reach across the aisle only to have my hand touched by something that has been so befouled that I will want to chop it off when I pull it back.

The reason I don't get along with Democrats anymore is because there really aren't any. The party has been hijacked by progressives.

The perpetually dishonest mainstream media has spent the last forty or so years telling the American public that conservatives hold sway in the GOP. If you want to get a laugh out of a real conservative, tell one of us that we have influence in the Republican party.

All the while the MSM has been crafting and perpetuating this narrative, the progressive fringe has been none-too-stealthily taking over the Democratic party. So much so that the last of the old guard Democrats had to rig their primary system to keep a communist from being their nominee in 2016. They've been exposed now, and all of the buzz about the potential Democratic field for 2020 centers around three progressives: Bernie Sanders, Elizabeth Warren, and Kamala Harris.

Sanders isn't even a full time Democrat, he just uses them during an election year so he can have a higher profile primary season. They're his toilet paper.

Barack Obama was, is, and always will be a progressive. He is a smarter politician than the current crop of far leftists among the Democrats, however. Obama was playing a long game. He's an advocate of single-payer health care, but he knew he couldn't get that passed, so he created a stepping stone to it in Obamacare.

The above-mentioned potential 2020 triumvirate are shrill, emotional politicians who all hope to be elected president solely by telling stupid people that the government will give them free stuff.

Even when they aren't lying about conservatives, they're lying about something.

I no longer have the patience to deal with people whose politics are based more on the spittle that forms at the corners of their mouths while ranting than on logic, history, or anything resembling common sense.

If you are a grown-up who still says that taxpayer-funded government programs provide "free" things then you are too stupid for me to waste precious breath talking to.

While I have no expectations whatsoever from the Republicans anymore, I expect nothing but the worst from progressives.

They never fail me.

My expectations game is pretty stress-free all around these days.

Third Beer. All day, every day.

**

Yes people, I know that my freedoms and yours are being assailed from the political left and that those tasked with fighting for them on the political right are too self-serving to see the big picture.

What this sojourn has taught me is that I haven't the slightest idea what to do about any of that. After so many years of pretending that I might be able to find out what to do and the hair-pulling frustration that brings about, I've opted for some surprisingly comforting realism.

Most will undoubtedly see this as acquiescence, if not outright surrender.

They will all be wrong.

I was affecting no change whatsoever before and I will be affecting no change whatsoever going forward. Same result, fewer headaches. Well, no headaches.

There is plenty of fight left in me, I am just not going to waste it on pissing in the wind just because that's what everybody else on "my side" is doing.

I am almost certain that the endgame the progressives have in mind involves a whole hell of a lot of civil unrest. That isn't going to be put off through polite political channels. Mitt Romney isn't your best weapon against Antifa, trust me.

That all seems like something for which I should rest.

Which I will do with this third beer that just arrived at my table.

About the Author

Stephen Kruiser is a professional stand-up comedian, political blogger and pundit. He lives in Tucson, AZ.

Made in the USA
Middletown, DE
29 January 2021